Water-Quality Data from Upper Klamath and Agency Lakes, Oregon, 2009–10

By D. Blake Eldridge, Sara L. Caldwell Eldridge, Liam N. Schenk, Dwight Q. Tanner, and Tamara M. Wood

Prepared in cooperation with the Bureau of Reclamation

Open-File Report 2012–1142

U.S. Department of the Interior
U.S. Geological Survey

U.S. Department of the Interior
KEN SALAZAR, Secretary

U.S. Geological Survey
Marcia K. McNutt, Director

U.S. Geological Survey, Reston, Virginia: 2012

For more information on the USGS—the Federal source for science about the Earth, its
natural and living resources, natural hazards, and the environment, visit http://www.usgs.gov
or call 1-888-ASK-USGS.

For an overview of USGS information products, including maps, imagery, and publications,
visit *http://www.usgs.gov/pubprod*

To order this and other USGS information products, visit *http://store.usgs.gov*

Suggested citation:
Eldridge. D.B., Caldwell Eldridge, S.L., Schenk, L.N., Tanner, D.Q., and Wood, T.M., 2012, Water-quality data from
Upper Klamath and Agency Lakes, Oregon, 2009–10: U.S. Geological Survey Open-File Report 2012–1142, 32 p.

Contents

Figures

Tables

Conversion Factors, Datums, and Abbreviations and Acronyms

Conversion Factors

Multiply	By	To obtain
liter (L)	1.057	quart (qt)
meter (m)	3.281	foot (ft)
meter per second (m/s)	3.281	foot per second (ft/s)
microgram per liter (μg/L)	1.0	part per billion (ppb)
micrometer (μm)	3.937×10^{-5}	inch (in)
milligram per liter (mg/L)	1.0	part per million (ppm)
milliliter (mL)	0.03382	fluid ounce (oz)
millimeter (mm)	0.03937	inch (in)
square kilometer (km^2)	0.3861	square mile (mi^2)

Temperature in degrees Celsius (°C) can be converted to degrees Fahrenheit (°F) as follows:
$$°F=(1.8 \times °C)+32.$$
Specific conductance is given in microsiemens per centimeter at 25 degrees Celsius (μS/cm at 25°C).

Datums

Vertical coordinate information is referenced to the Bureau of Reclamation datum, which is 1.78 feet above National Geodetic Vertical Datum of 1929 (NGVD 29).

Horizontal coordinate information is referenced to the North American Datum of 1927 (NAD 27).

Elevation, as used in this report, refers to the vertical distance above the Bureau of Reclamation datum.

Abbreviations and Acronyms

Abbreviation or Acronym	Definition
ACS	American Chemical Society
ADAPS	Automated Data Processing System
AFA	*Aphanizomenon flos-aquae*
BRPNL	Bureau of Reclamation Pacific-Northwest Regional Laboratory
CBL	Chesapeake Biological Laboratory
DOC	dissolved organic carbon
MRL	minimum reporting level
NWIS	National Water Information System
NWQL	National Water Quality Laboratory
ORWSC	Oregon Water Science Center
SRWQL	Sprague River Water Quality Laboratory
USGS	U.S. Geological Survey

Water-Quality Data from Upper Klamath and Agency Lakes, Oregon, 2009–10

By D. Blake Eldridge, Sara L. Caldwell Eldridge, Liam N. Schenk, Dwight Q. Tanner, and Tamara M. Wood

Significant Findings

The U.S. Geological Survey Upper Klamath Lake water-quality monitoring program collected data from multiparameter continuous water-quality monitors, weekly water-quality samples, and meteorological stations during 2009 and 2010 from May through November each year. The results of these measurements and sample analyses, as well as quality-control data for the water-quality samples, are presented in this report for 14 sites on Upper Klamath Lake and 2 sites on Agency Lake. These 2 years of data demonstrate a contrast in the seasonal bloom of the dominant cyanobacterium, *Aphanizomenon flos-aquae*, that can be related to differences in the measured water quality and meteorological variables. Some of the significant findings from 2009 and 2010 are listed below.

- Both 2009 and 2010 were characterized by two cyanobacteria blooms, but the blooms differed in timing and intensity. The first bloom in 2009 peaked in late June and at higher chlorophyll *a* concentrations at most sites than the first bloom in 2010, which peaked in mid-July. A major decline in the first 2009 bloom occurred in late July and was followed by a second bloom that peaked at most sites in mid-August and persisted through September. The decline of the weaker first bloom in 2010 occurred in early August and was followed by a more substantial second bloom that peaked between late August and early September at most sites.

- Dissolved oxygen minima associated with bloom declines occurred approximately 2 weeks earlier in 2009 (mid-July) than in 2010 (early August). pH maxima associated with rapid bloom growth occurred in late June and again in mid-August in 2009 and in mid-July and late August in 2010.

- In both years, the maxima for total phosphorus and total nitrogen concentrations coincided with the chlorophyll *a* maximum. The maxima for dissolved nutrient concentrations (orthophosphate, ammonia, and nitrite plus nitrate) coincided with the declines of the first blooms.

- Total particulate carbon, total particulate nitrogen, and total particulate phosphorus concentrations were measured in 2009 only. The ratios of carbon to phosphorus and nitrogen to phosphorus in particulates were the highest of the entire season during the rapid growth phase of the first bloom and were the lowest of the season during the decline of the first bloom. These ratios increased with the onset of the second bloom in that year, but to a lesser degree.

- Meteorological data show that 2009 was warmer (particularly in June and July), less windy, and more humid early in the season than 2010. The difference in water temperatures reflected the difference in air temperatures in that the lakes were warmer in 2009 than in 2010 starting in early May, when the sensors were deployed, through most of June. Water temperature peaked at a higher value in 2009, and there were more clear days in June 2009 than in June 2010.

Introduction

Background

Severe water-quality problems in Upper Klamath Lake (fig. 1) led to the listing of Lost River suckers (*Deltistes luxatus*) and shortnose suckers (*Chasmistes brevirostris*) as endangered in 1988 (Stubbs and White, 1993). In addition to several periods of high mortality, low rates of recruitment from the juvenile to the spawning adult stages in these fish populations have also been noted (Janney and others, 2008). This change in the sucker age demographic may be linked to poor water quality associated with phytoplankton growth and fluctuations in water chemistry. Since the construction of the Link River Dam (fig. 1) in 1921 and other anthropogenic changes to the surrounding watershed, hypereutrophication of Upper Klamath Lake has caused the phytoplankton community in the lake to shift to a near monoculture of the cyanobacterium *Aphanizomenon flos-aquae* (AFA) during the summer (Kann, 1998; Perkins and others, 2000). Massive blooms and subsequent declines in abundance of the phytoplankton directly coincide with episodes of high pH (> 9), widely variable and often extreme dissolved oxygen concentrations (anoxic to supersaturated), and high un-ionized ammonia concentrations (> 0.5 mg/L as N; Hoilman and others, 2008; Lindenberg and others, 2009). Large AFA blooms and the accompanying degraded water-quality conditions also occur annually in Agency Lake, although the intensity and duration of such conditions usually differ from those in Upper Klamath Lake.

The U.S. Geological Survey (USGS), in cooperation with the Bureau of Reclamation, began monitoring Upper Klamath Lake water quality in 2002 (table 1). From 2002 through 2004, continuous monitoring was limited to the northern part of the lake in support of USGS telemetry tracking of endangered adult suckers (Wood and others, 2006). These 3 years of monitoring showed that the timing and severity of poor water-quality conditions in Upper Klamath Lake were highly variable from year to year. However, in each year, seasonal patterns of low dissolved-oxygen concentrations and high pH were well correlated with the dynamics of annual AFA blooms, and seasonally low dissolved-oxygen concentrations often occurred with the decline of the first AFA bloom. High fish mortality in 2003 was associated with a particularly severe low dissolved-oxygen event that coincided with a bloom decline at the end of July (Banish and others, 2009).

In 2005, the USGS water-quality monitoring program expanded for Upper Klamath Lake and added monitoring sites in Agency Lake (table 1). Meteorological stations were established around the shoreline of Upper Klamath Lake, in addition to the two floating rafts used in previous years, to provide greater spatial resolution of wind data for a hydrodynamic model (Wood and others, 2008; Hoilman and others, 2008). These stations also collected air temperature, relative humidity, and solar radiation data for use in a heat transport model (Wood and others, 2008). Monitoring in 2005 included 15 continuous water-quality monitors at 13 sites in Upper Klamath Lake and 2 monitors in Agency Lake that recorded hourly water temperature, pH, specific conductance, and dissolved oxygen concentration or percent saturation. At three sites in Upper Klamath Lake, where the depth was greater than 4 m, monitors were deployed at 1 m below the water surface and at 1 m above the lake bottom. At six sites, MDN, WMR, EPT, MDT, HDB, and MDL, light- and dark-bottle experiments were conducted to measure oxygen production and consumption (Hoilman and others, 2008). Samples to be analyzed for chlorophyll *a* and nutrients were also collected at these six sites. The results of the monitoring program in 2005 are summarized and interpretation of the data is provided in Hoilman and others (2008).

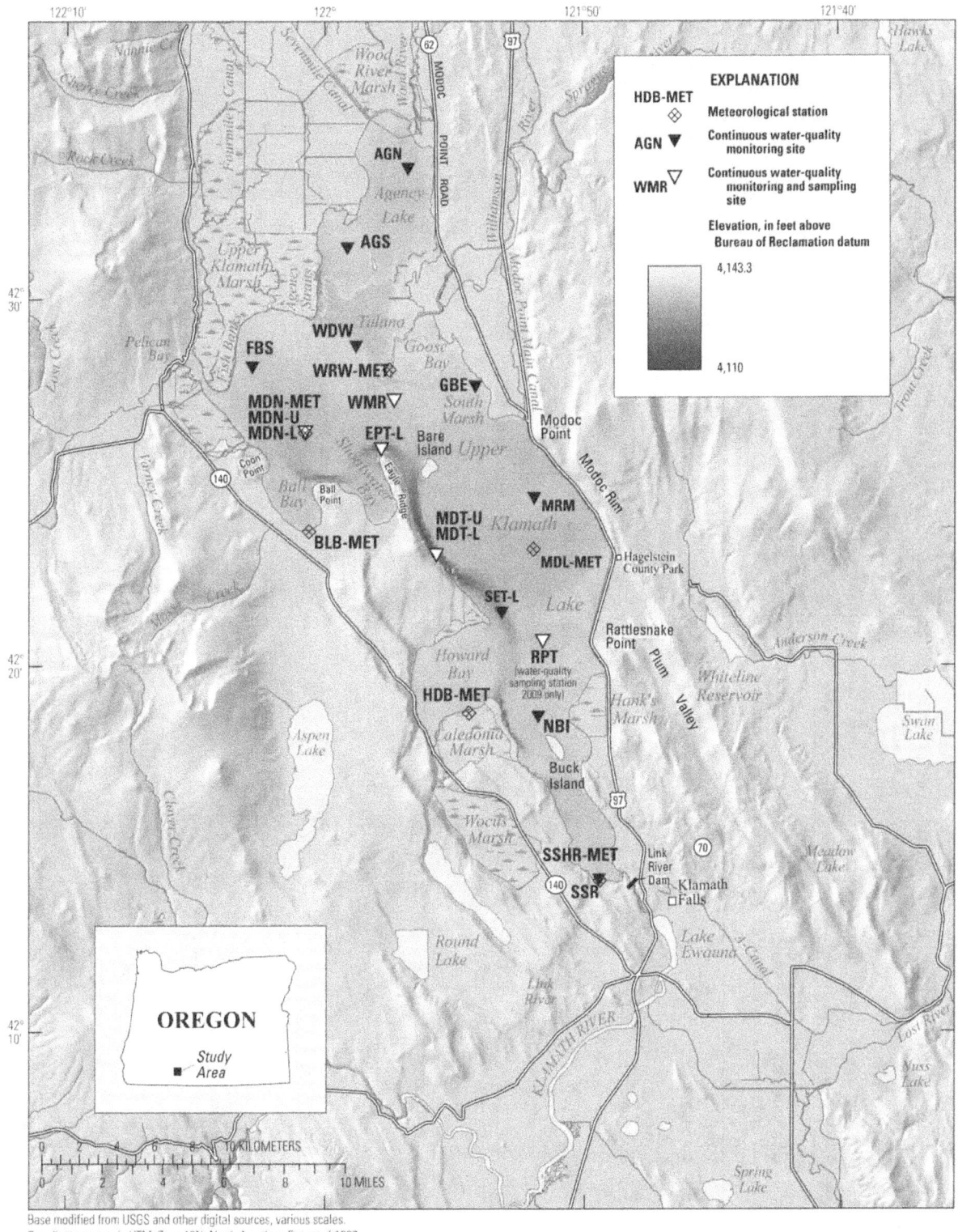

Figure 1. Map showing location of meteorological (MET) sites, continuous water-quality monitoring sites, and continuous water-quality monitoring and sampling sites, Upper Klamath and Agency Lakes, Oregon, 2009–10. Continuous monitoring and sampling site descriptions are shown in table 2, and meteorological station descriptions are shown in table 3.

Table 1. Summary of U.S. Geological Survey monitoring studies on Upper Klamath Lake, Oregon, since 2002.

[Dissolved nutrients include ammonium, orthophosphate, and nitrite plus nitrate in all years. Although some years have the same number of continuous monitoring and/or water sampling sites, the locations of these sites may have changed. The number of continuous monitoring sites in Upper Klamath and Agency Lakes is shown. Phaeophytin *a* concentrations were also measured in all chlorophyll *a* samples but are not included in the table for simplicity. Floating meteorological stations were located at sites MDN and MDL between 2006 and 2010. DO, dissolved oxygen; SC, specific conductance; UKL, Upper Klamath Lake; Agency, Agency Lake; DOC, dissolved organic carbon; TSS, total suspended solids; RH, relative humidity]

Study year	Number of continuous monitoring sites	Continuously monitored parameters	Number, location of sampling sites	Parameters measured in water samples	Number of meteorological stations	Meteorological data (number of sites)	Additional data	Reference(s)
2002	11	pH, DO, temperature, SC	4, Northern UKL	chlorophyll *a*, total phosphorus, dissolved nutrients	2 Floating (profiling buoys)	Air temperature (1), Wind speed, direction (2), RH (1)	Profiling buoy at 2 sites	Wood and others, 2006
2003	14	pH, DO, temperature, SC	3, Northern UKL	chlorophyll *a*, total phosphorus, dissolved nutrients	2 Floating (profiling buoys)	Air temperature (1), Wind speed, direction (2), RH (1)	Profiling buoy at 2 sites	Wood and others, 2006
2004	14	pH, DO, temperature, SC	4, Northern UKL	chlorophyll *a*, total phosphorus, dissolved nutrients	2 Floating (profiling buoys)	Air temperature (1), Wind speed, direction (2), RH (1)	Profiling buoy at 2 sites	Wood and others, 2006
2005	15	pH, DO, temperature, SC	6, UKL (lakewide); 2, Agency	chlorophyll *a*, total phosphorus, dissolved nutrients	4 Land-based; 2 Floating (profiling buoys)	Air temperature (3), Wind speed, direction (6), RH (3), Solar radiation (1)	DO production, consumption	Hoilman and others, 2008
2006	19	pH, DO, temperature, SC	6, UKL (lakewide); 2, Agency	chlorophyll *a*, total phosphorus, total nitrogen, dissolved nutrients	4 Land-based; 2 Floating (sites MDN, MDL)	Air temperature (5), Wind speed, direction (6), RH (5), Solar radiation (2)	DO production, consumption	Lindenberg and others, 2009
2007	19	pH, DO, temperature, SC	6, UKL (lakewide); 2, Agency	chlorophyll *a*, total phosphorus, total nitrogen, dissolved nutrients, DOC	6 Land-based; 2 Floating (sites MDN, MDL)	Air temperature (7), Wind speed, direction (8), RH (7), Solar radiation (4)	Microcystins, cylindro-spermopsins	Kannarr and others, 2010; Eldridge and others, 2012
2008	19	pH, DO, temperature, SC	4, UKL (lakewide); 2, Agency	chlorophyll *a*, total phosphorus, total nitrogen, dissolved nutrients	6 Land-based; 2 Floating (sites MDN, MDL)	Air temperature (7), Wind speed, direction (8), RH (7), Solar radiation (4)	Microcystins, cylindro-spermopsins	Kannarr and others, 2010; Eldridge and others, 2012
2009	14	pH, DO, temperature, SC	5, UKL (lakewide); 2, Agency	chlorophyll *a*, total phosphorus, total nitrogen, dissolved nutrients, total particulate nutrients, TSS	4 Land-based; 2 Floating (sites MDN, MDL)	Air temperature (6), Wind speed, direction (6), RH (6), Solar radiation (2)	Microcystins	Current study; Eldridge and others, 2012
2010	14	pH, DO, temperature, SC	4, UKL (lakewide); 2, Agency	chlorophyll *a*, total phosphorus, total nitrogen, dissolved nutrients	4 Land-based; 2 Floating (sites MDN, MDL)	Air temperature (6), Wind speed, direction (6), RH (6), Solar radiation (2)	Microcystins	Current study; Eldridge and others, 2012

In 2006, 23 continuous monitors were deployed at 19 sites in the open waters of Upper Klamath and Agency Lakes, but the locations of some sites were changed (table 1). Monitors were added at four new sites located 5–10 m from the shoreline of Upper Klamath Lake, and three sites were removed or consolidated. Light- and dark-bottle experiments and weekly water samplings for the analyses of chlorophyll *a* and nutrients were continued at the same six sites as in 2005. The results of the monitoring program in 2006 are summarized and interpretation of the data is provided in Lindenberg and others (2009).

Continuous monitoring sites and meteorological stations in Agency Lake and in the open waters of Upper Klamath Lake were the same in 2007 and 2008 as in 2006 (two nearshore sites used in 2006 were moved in 2007). Water samples were collected at the continuous monitoring sites MDT, EPT, MDN, RPT (2007 only), WMR, and HDB (2007 only). In 2007, the collection of samples for the determination of the concentration of dissolved organic carbon concentration was added to monitor conditions prior to and during the weeks following the breaching of levees at the Williamson River Delta. In addition, the 2007 sampling season was extended into November, and samples were collected until mid-October in 2008. The results of monitoring in 2007 and 2008 are summarized in Kannarr and others (2010).

The long-term monitoring effort that began in 2005 continued in 2009–10 with some changes. This report presents the results of the 2009–10 data-collection program, including data from continuous water-quality monitors, laboratory analyses of water samples, and data from meteorological stations. In both years, 16 continuous water-quality monitors were operated at 14 sites in Upper Klamath Lake and Agency Lake, 5 fewer sites than in 2006–2008. The number of meteorological stations remained the same as in 2005 and 2006. In 2009, water samples were collected weekly for the analyses of chlorophyll *a*, total nutrients, dissolved nutrients, total particulate nutrients, total particulate carbon,

and total suspended solids (TSS) from five continuous monitor sites, MDT, EPT, MDN, RPT, and WMR. Weekly water samples for the analyses of chlorophyll *a*, total nutrients, and dissolved nutrients were collected from four sites, MDT, EPT, MDN, and WMR in 2010 (water samples were not analyzed for total particulate carbon and nutrients in 2010). In 2009, the weekly collection of cyanotoxin (microcystins and cylindrospermopsins) data was added to the program (samples were collected less frequently for cyanotoxin analysis in 2007 and 2008). Those data are not discussed here, but are presented in Eldridge and others (2012).

Description of Study Area

Upper Klamath Lake (fig. 1) is located in a broad structural graben in south-central Oregon. Much of its 9,415-km^2 drainage basin is composed of volcanic deposits. The lake is large and shallow, with a surface area of 232 km^2 and an average depth of 2.8 m. The water depth throughout most of the lake (about 90 percent) is less than 4 m; however, a narrow trench runs parallel to Eagle Ridge on the lake's western shore, which has a full-pool depth of approximately 15 m at the deepest point. Agency Lake, just north of Upper Klamath Lake, adds about 38 km^2 of surface area to the Upper Klamath Lake–Agency Lake hydrologic system (Johnson, 1985). Agency Lake is also shallow, with a maximum depth of about 3 m and an average depth of 0.9 m. The largest single source of inflow to the lake is the mostly groundwater-fed Williamson River, which contributes nearly one-half, on an annual average, of incoming water (Hubbard, 1970) and enters Upper Klamath Lake near its northern end. Other tributaries to the system include the Wood River, Fourmile Canal, and Sevenmile Canal, which enter Agency Lake at its northern end (fig. 1).

Upper Klamath Lake is a natural water body, but lake-surface elevation has been regulated since 1921, when the Link River dam (fig. 1) was completed at the southern outlet of the lake. The dam is operated by the Bureau of Reclamation.

The lake is now the primary water source for the Bureau of Reclamation's Klamath Project, an irrigation system developed to supply water to farms and ranches in and around the Upper Klamath Basin (Bureau of Reclamation, 2000).

Prior to autumn 2007, Agency Lake was connected to Upper Klamath Lake by a narrow channel (Agency Straits), but in October 2007 levees surrounding the Tulana Farms portion of the Williamson River Delta (fig. 1) were breached as part of a major restoration project (Wong and others, 2010). In November 2008, levees around the Goose Bay portion of the delta were breached, and the current landscape configuration around the delta was created. Water can now move between Agency Lake and Upper Klamath Lake across the delta. The 2009 monitoring season is the first in which the shoreline around the two lakes incorporated the entire restored area of the delta.

Methods

Continuous Water-Quality Monitors

Two YSI model 600XLM continuous water-quality monitors ("sondes") were deployed at 2 sites in Agency Lake, and 14 sondes were deployed at 12 sites in Upper Klamath Lake (2 sondes each were deployed at sites MDT and MDN; fig. 1, table 2). In Upper Klamath and Agency Lakes, 13 sondes were at 11 open-water sites (more than 10 m from shore), and 3 sondes were at 3 nearshore sites (5–10 m from shore or in reed beds adjacent to open water). All sondes recorded depth, dissolved oxygen concentration and percent saturation, pH, specific conductance, and water temperature at the beginning of every hour. Data were telemetered from a single site, MDN, in 2009 and 2010.

Table 2. Continuous water-quality monitoring and sampling sites, Upper Klamath and Agency Lakes, Oregon, 2009–10.

[Locations of sites are shown in figure 1. Sites are listed in order of decreasing depth. Vertical coordinate information is referenced to the Bureau of Reclamation datum, which is 1.78 feet above the National Geodetic Vertical Datum of 1929 (NGVD 29). Horizontal coordinate information is referenced to the North American Datum of 1927 (NAD 27)]

Site name	Site name abbreviation	USGS site identification no.	Latitude (north)	Longitude (west)	Full-pool measured depth (meters)
Open-water sites					
Middle of trench (lower)	MDT-L	422305121553800	42°23'5.1"	121°55'38.2"	15.0
Middle of trench (upper)	MDT-U	422305121553803	42°23'5.1"	121°55'38.2"	15.0
Eagle Point (lower)	EPT-L	422559121574400	42°25'59.2"	121°57'44.1"	12.5
South end of trench (lower)	SET-L	422128121530600	42°21'27.8"	121°53'05.9"	7.0
Midnorth (lower)	MDN-L	422622122004000	42°26'21.5"	122°00'40.0"	4.2
Midnorth (upper)	MDN-U	422622122004003	42°26'21.5"	122°00'40.0"	4.2
Modoc Rim	MRM	422437121515200	42°24'37.3"	121°51'52.4"	3.7
Rattlesnake Point	RPT	422042121513100	42°20'41.6"	121°51'31.4"	3.4
Agency North	AGN	423335121564300	42°33'35.0"	121°56'43.0"	3.0
Fish Banks	FBS	422808122024400	42°28'08.8"	122°02'43.5"	2.8

Table 2. Continuous water-quality monitoring and sampling sites, Upper Klamath and Agency Lakes, Oregon, 2009–10.—continued

[Locations of sites are shown in figure 1. Sites are listed in order of decreasing depth. Vertical coordinate information is referenced to the Bureau of Reclamation datum, which is 1.78 feet above the National Geodetic Vertical Datum of 1929 (NGVD 29). Horizontal coordinate information is referenced to the North American Datum of 1927 (NAD 27)]

Site name	Site name abbreviation	USGS site identification no.	Latitude (north)	Longitude (west)	Full-pool measured depth (meters)
Open-water sites					
North Buck Island	NBI	421838121513900	42°18'38.0"	121°51'39.0"	2.8
Williamson River outlet	WMR	422719121571400	42°27'19.4"	121°57'13.6"	2.5
Agency South	AGS	423124121583400	42°31'24.9"	121°59'03.4"	2.5
Nearshore sites					
South Shore	SSR	421410121492000	42°14'10.0"	121°49'20.0"	2.5
Goose Bay East	GBE	422739121540800	42°27'38.8"	121°54' 7.5"	2.4
Williamson Delta West	WDW	422842121584300	42°28'41.9"	121°58'43.4"	2.2

Sondes at most sites were placed horizontally in the water column 1 m from the lake bottom. Placing the sondes horizontally avoids sensor contact with the lake bottom in windy conditions and ensures that the depth sensor is located near the same depth as the other sensors, which are approximately 0.15 m below it on the sonde. At sites with a water depth of less than 2 m, sondes were placed at the midpoint of the water column. The sonde depth of 1 m from the lake bottom was selected to provide data relevant to the bottom-dwelling suckers. At MDN only, one sonde was installed vertically at 1 m between the sensors (pH, dissolved oxygen, and specific conductance) and the lake bottom, and another sonde was placed at 1 m between the sensors and the water surface to avoid damage to attached communication cables that were used for data telemetry. In addition, two sondes were placed horizontally on the same mooring at fixed depths of 1 m from the lake surface and at 1 m from the sediment at MDT to monitor water-quality conditions near the water surface and to provide comparisons to conditions near the lake bottom.

Quality control of the data was determined by field information collected during weekly site visits and by processing the time series according to the procedures described in Wagner and others (2006). During site visits, sondes were cleaned and the depths at which they were located in the water column were confirmed. Prior to each cleaning, field measurements of dissolved oxygen concentration, pH, specific conductance, and temperature at the depth of the site sonde were recorded with a newly calibrated reference sonde to assess the site sonde's performance. Site sondes were deployed for approximately 3 weeks before being replaced. After retrieval, the calibration of each site sonde was evaluated to measure calibration drift during deployment. The raw continuous data from site sondes were uploaded to the USGS automated data-processing system (ADAPS). Corrections to data due to biological fouling and calibration drift were calculated and applied in ADAPS according to Wagner and others (2006).

Collection of Water-Quality Samples

Water samples were collected weekly between May 20, 2009, and September 28, 2009, and between May 12, 2010, and September 27, 2010, according to established sampling protocols (U.S. Geological Survey, variously dated). Samples were analyzed for concentrations of total phosphorus, total nitrogen, chlorophyll *a*, phaeophytin *a,* and dissolved nutrients: ammonia plus ammonium (hereafter referred to as ammonia), orthophosphate, and nitrite plus nitrate. Additionally, 2009 samples were analyzed for total suspended solids, total particulate carbon, total particulate nitrogen, total particulate phosphorus, particulate inorganic carbon, and particulate inorganic phosphorous. Sampling was conducted at the continuous water-quality monitoring sites MDT, EPT, MDN, and WMR in 2009 and 2010 and also at RPT in 2009 only (fig. 1; RPT was not sampled in 2010).

Water samples to be analyzed for total phosphorus, total nitrogen, chlorophyll *a*, and phaeophytin *a* were collected by integrating equal amounts of water over the depth of the water column (depth integration). Depth-integrated samples were collected in two 2-L polyethylene bottles held in a weighted cage. Bottle caps with two small ports, one for the inflow of water and another for the escape of displaced air, were used. The cage and sample bottles were lowered at a constant rate through the water column to within 0.5 m from the bottom at sites less than 10.5 m ("shallow" sites: MDN, WMR, and RPT). At sites greater than 10.5 m ("deep" sites: EPT and MDT), samples were collected to a depth of 10 m in order to assure the integrity of the depth integration (sample collection bottles may fill completely before reaching the surface when sampling at depths greater than 10 m, which would prevent the sample from being collected evenly over the entire sampled depth). The contents of sample bottles from multiple collections at each site were composited and mixed in a churn splitter prior to filling analysis bottles.

Water samples analyzed for dissolved nutrients (ammonia, orthophosphate, and nitrite plus nitrate), total suspended solids (TSS), total particulate carbon (TPC), particulate inorganic carbon (PIC), total particulate nitrogen (TPN), total particulate phosphorous (TPP), and particulate inorganic phosphorous (PIP) were collected from a point mid-depth in the water column at shallow sites. At deep sites, water was collected at two points in the water column (at one-quarter and three-quarters of the total depth). Samples were collected by lowering one end of the sample tubing fixed to a sonde to the appropriate depth in the water column, and lake water was pumped to the surface with a peristaltic pump. After purging the tubing for 2 minutes with lake water, unfiltered samples for TSS, TPC, PIC, TPN, TPP, and PIP analyses were collected. Samples for dissolved nutrient analyses were filtered through a 0.45-μm capsule filter connected to the outflow end of the tubing.

All water samples were chilled on site and during transport. Total phosphorus and total nitrogen samples were preserved immediately after collection with the addition of 1 mL of 4.5 normal (4.5 N) sulfuric acid. Dissolved nutrient, total phosphorus, and total nitrogen samples were analyzed at the Sprague River Water Quality Laboratory (SRWQL) in Chiloquin, Oregon. Dissolved nutrient samples were analyzed using USGS methods I-2525-89 and I-2522-90 for ammonia, I-2545-90 for nitrite plus nitrate, and I-2606-89 and I-2601-90 for orthophosphate (Fishman, 1993). Concentrations of ammonia in the un-ionized form (NH_3) were determined from tabulated percentages of un-ionized ammonia as a function of pH and temperature (U.S. Environmental Protection Agency, 1979a) and the measured concentrations of ammonia plus ammonium in water samples. Total phosphorous and total nitrogen samples were analyzed using USGS method I-4650-03 (Patton and Kryskalla, 2003). Water samples collected for chlorophyll *a* and phaeophytin *a* analyses were passed through 47-mm-diameter, 1.2-μm pore size, glass-fiber (GF/F) filters (Whatman, Inc., Piscataway, New

Jersey) at the USGS Klamath Falls Field Station and immediately frozen. These samples were stored and analyzed according to Standard Method 10200H (American Public Health Association, 2005) at the Bureau of Reclamation Pacific-Northwest Regional Laboratory (BRPNL) in Boise, Idaho.

Water samples for TSS, TPC, TPP, TPN, PIP, and PIC analyses were collected in 2009 only. Samples for TPC, TPN, and PIC analyses were filtered at the Klamath Falls Field Station using pre-combusted 25-mm-diameter, 0.7-μm pore size, glass fiber filters (GF/F). Lake water collected for TSS, TPP, and PIP analyses was filtered using 47-mm-diameter, 0.7-μm pore size, GF/F (filters used for TSS analysis were pre-weighed). All filtered samples were immediately frozen and shipped to the University of Maryland Chesapeake Biological Laboratory (CBL) in Solomons, Maryland, for analysis. TPC, TPN, and PIC samples were analyzed according to U.S. Environmental Protection Agency method 440.0 (Zimmerman and others, 1997). TPP and PIP samples were analyzed according to Aspila and others (1976). TSS is the retained material on a tared glass filter pad after filtration of a well-mixed sample of water (U.S. Environmental Protection Agency, 1979b; American Public Health Association, 2005). Data from all laboratories were archived in the USGS National Water Information System (NWIS).

Meteorological Sites

The locations of meteorological sites are shown in figure 1 and listed in table 3. Wind-speed and direction data were collected by R.M. Young™ model 05103-5 wind monitors at a height of 3 m at the land-based sites and at a height of 2 m at the floating sites. Campbell Scientific® CS215 or HMP35C relative humidity and air-temperature sensors collected air temperature and relative humidity data at a height of 2 m at the land-based sites and at a height of 1.5 m at the floating sites. Additionally, solar-radiation data were collected at WRW-MET using a Li-Cor LI200SZ pyranometer and at SSHR-MET using an Eppley Laboratory Precision Spectral Pyranometer (PSP) and a Precision Infrared Radiometer (PIR). The PSP measures solar irradiance (shortwave radiation), whereas the PIR measures incoming atmospheric irradiance (longwave radiation). Data collected from all sensors at a site were collected and stored every 10 minutes by a Campbell Scientific CR510, CR10, or CR10X data logger. A 12-volt battery charged by a solar-power array provided power to each site. Data were retrieved from the data loggers during site visits approximately every 2 weeks during the field season. During these visits, sensors were cleaned and checked for catastrophic problems by comparison with hand-held sensors. Raw meteorological data were loaded into ADAPS and processed in a similar manner as the water-quality monitor data.

Table 3. Meteorological sites and parameters measured, Upper Klamath Lake, Oregon, 2009–10.

[Site locations are shown in figure 1.]

Meteorological site name	Site name abbreviation	USGS site identification no.	Latitude (north)	Longitude (west)	Parameters measured
Midnorth[1]	MDN-MET	422622122004000	42°26'21.5"	122°00'40.0"	Wind speed and direction, air temperature, relative humidity
Williamson River West	WRW-MET	422807121572500	42°28'7.1"	121°57'25.0"	Wind speed and direction, air temperature, relative humidity, solar radiation
Ball Bay	BLB-MET	422341122003800	42°23'40.9"	122°00'38.4"	Wind speed and direction, air temperature, relative humidity

Table 3. Meteorological sites and parameters measured, Upper Klamath Lake, Oregon, 2009–10.—continued

[Site locations are shown in figure 1.]

Meteorological site name	Site name abbreviation	USGS site identification no.	Latitude (north)	Longitude (west)	Parameters measured
Midlake[1]	MDL-MET	422312121515900	42°23'12.0"	121°51'59.1"	Wind speed and direction, air temperature, relative humidity
Howard Bay	HDB-MET	421846121542800	42°18'46.2"	121°54'28.0"	Wind speed and direction, air temperature, relative humidity
South Shore	SSHR-MET	421402121491400	42°14'02.76"	121°49'14.38"	Wind speed and direction, air temperature, relative humidity, solar radiation

[1]Floating site

Data Processing

Lakewide daily median values were calculated from data received from continuous water-quality monitors. The values were calculated from 24 hourly measurements made at all eligible open-water Upper Klamath Lake sites combined. Prior to calculating daily median values, data from water-quality monitors were screened using temporal and spatial criteria. At least 19 of 24 hourly measurements from a site on a given day had to be present for the site to be included in the lakewide calculation for that day. In addition, to apply the spatial criterion, at least 9 of the 11 continuous monitor sites had to have enough data to be included in the calculation of each daily median. At sites in Agency Lake, the data were not combined, but at least 20 of 24 hourly measurements had to be present in order to calculate the daily median.

For statistics at individual meteorological sites, the temporal criterion required that at least 20 of 24 hourly measurements made in one day were present in order to calculate the daily median. Air-temperature, relative humidity, wind speed, and wind direction data were collected at six sites, and those data were combined to calculate a lakewide daily median. Data from at least five of the six sites had to be included in order to compute a lakewide daily median. Solar-radiation data were collected at only two sites (SSHR and WRW), and those data were not combined before calculating a daily median.

Quality Control

Quality-control samples were collected at site MDN for all sample types in 2009 and 2010. These samples included a field equipment blank (the first sample collected every week) for total phosphorus, total nitrogen, dissolved nutrients, total particulate nutrients (2009 only), and total particulate carbon (2009 only); a laboratory blank for particulate nutrient (2009 only), particulate carbon (2009 only), and chlorophyll *a* samples; and either a sequential replicate sample (hereafter referred to as a "replicate" sample) or a split replicate sample (hereafter referred to as a "split" sample). Blank spike and sample matrix spike samples were also collected twice each year for total and dissolved nutrient analyses to measure bias in the analytical procedures used by SRWQL. Blank spike samples were used as standard reference samples in that they provided a point of comparison for the sample matrix spikes, which were used to measure site- and situation-dependent bias in analyzing the environmental samples.

Field equipment blanks consisted of American Chemical Society (ACS) reagent-grade inorganic blank water processed onsite through clean sampling equipment prior to processing environmental samples. Laboratory blanks for chlorophyll *a*, phaeophytin *a*, and total particulate nutrients were collected using ACS reagent-grade inorganic blank water processed in the laboratory through a clean filter and filtering apparatus prior to processing environmental samples. Total particulate carbon laboratory blanks were collected from pesticide-grade (organic) blank water. The filter membranes were frozen and sent for analysis with environmental samples. Analysis of blank samples determines if equipment cleaning, sample collection and handling, sample storage and processing, sample analysis, sample transport, and collection equipment cause measurable contamination to environmental samples.

Replicate and split samples were collected on alternating weeks throughout the sampling period and submitted to SRWQL, BRPNL, and CBL. Spike samples were collected twice during the sample season and submitted blindly to SRWQL. SRWQL participates in the USGS Standard Reference Sample Project, which compares laboratories nationwide for quality control. In addition, samples for quality control analyses submitted to SRWQL and BRPNL were evaluated according to the USGS Branch of Quality Systems Laboratory Evaluation Project (BQS LEP) to validate the use of these laboratories in the Upper Klamath Lake long-term water-quality monitoring project. The SRWQL (BQS laboratory 697) evaluation began May 2007, and the Bureau of Reclamation (BQS laboratory 746) evaluation began November 2008. CBL is currently being evaluated. Results of both BQS LEP projects indicate that the laboratory methods, performance data, and concentration ranges of submitted samples are appropriate and applicable to the ongoing Upper Klamath Lake monitoring study. Replicate environmental samples were collected twice in rapid succession from the same location (the entire sample collection procedure was completed twice) and analyzed to determine variability of the system, variability of collection, and variability in the analytical methods. Split samples are environmental samples collected once and divided into two or more samples (analysis bottles were filled sequentially from the same churn) to determine the variability in

sample splitting and in the analytical methods. Although replicate samples measure all variability in field and laboratory procedures, split samples were collected in addition to replicates to isolate sources of analytical variability. This allows the determination of how much variability is due to sampling versus analysis. Spike samples were prepared at the USGS Klamath Falls Field Station by adding target compounds (a field-matrix spike mixture) to ACS reagent-grade inorganic blank water and to environmental samples collected concurrently with non-spiked samples. In addition, interlaboratory split samples were collected twice each year and submitted to SRWQL, BRPNL, CBL, the USGS National Water Quality Laboratory (NWQL), Aquatic Research, Inc., Seattle, Washington, and the USGS Oregon Water Science Center, Portland, Oregon (ORWSC; for chlorophyll *a* only) to determine variability in the analytical methods used by these laboratories.

In 2009, the percentage of blank samples with concentrations larger than the minimum reporting level (MRL) was 10 percent or less for most analytes. The two exceptions were total particulate carbon, with 31 percent of field blank samples exceeding the MRL, and ammonia, with 55 percent of field blank samples exceeding the MRL (appendix A, table A1). Concentrations of particulate carbon in environmental samples were typically larger than the concentrations detected in the blanks, as the 10th percentile of environmental samples was 0.67 mg/L and the median was 3.37 mg/L. In contrast to the environmental sample concentrations, the median concentration in particulate carbon blank field samples above the minimum reporting limit was 0.12 mg/L, and the concentrations of 90 percent of these samples were below 0.19 mg/L. Therefore, low-level contamination indicated by the blanks did not limit the use of these data. Most concentrations of ammonia in the environmental samples were larger than the concentrations detected in the blanks. The median value of the ammonia field blank samples with concentrations greater than the minimum reporting limit was 0.013 mg/L, and 90 percent of these samples had concentrations below 0.021 mg/L (the 90th percentile). However, these concentrations were minimal when compared with concentrations in the environmental samples, in that the 10th percentile of the environmental samples was 0.016 mg/L and the median was 0.11 mg/L. Therefore, contamination did not substantially limit the use of the data.

The split and replicate samples for 2009 (appendix A, tables A2 and A3) showed mean relative percent differences less than 20 percent, with the exception of the total particulate split samples for carbon, nitrogen, and phosphorus and the replicate samples for total particulate carbon, particulate inorganic phosphorus, and total suspended solids. This difference in the majority of split and replicate samples generally agrees with results of previous quality-control sampling in this long-term monitoring program (total particulate nutrient and carbon samples were collected only in 2009; Hoilman and others, 2008; Lindenberg and others, 2009; Kannarr and others, 2010). Between 2005 and 2008, the median difference between most split or replicate samples did not exceed 15 percent (chlorophyll *a* and phaeophytin *a* samples collected in 2007 were determined to be of poor quality and, therefore, not reported). However, in 2008, the median differences between split phaeophytin *a* samples, split chlorophyll *a* samples, and replicate chlorophyll *a* samples were between 20 and 25 percent, while replicate phaeophytin *a* varied by 39 percent. The particulate analyses, conducted in 2009, were of solid samples, so more variability is expected in the subsampling procedure compared to liquid samples. The coefficients of variation for most interlaboratory split samples were less than 30 percent, which is similar to results from between 2006 and 2008 (the interlaboratory split analysis was not performed in 2005, and the analysis was performed only once in 2007). In 2009, three sets of interlaboratory split samples, for ammonia, total particulate carbon, and total particulate

nitrogen concentrations, had coefficients of variation above 30 percent (appendix A, table A4). The ammonia split on September 14, 2009, had a 48-percent coefficient of variation when the mean of the sample concentrations was 19.7 µg/L. However, on July 21, 2009, the split among the same laboratories showed a coefficient of variation of 5 percent when the mean of the sample concentrations was 933 µg/L, indicating more analytical variability at the lower concentration. The interlaboratory splits of total particulate carbon and nitrogen on July 21, 2009, had coefficients of variation of 57 and 63 percent, respectively, when the mean concentrations in the samples were 538 µg/L for total particulate carbon and 95.4 µg/L for total particulate nitrogen. On September 14, 2009, the coefficients of variation were 4 percent for total particulate carbon and nitrogen when the mean concentration of the samples was approximately an order of magnitude higher, also indicating more analytical variability at lower concentrations.

Bias measured by analysis of spike samples is known as "recovery," which is a measure of analyte in a sample expressed as the percentage of the spiked amount (U.S. Geological Survey, 2006). The recovery in a sample without loss or gain of the measured analyte (due to degradation or matrix character) should be 100 percent. In 2009, mean nutrient spike recoveries ranged between 72 and 122 percent (appendix A, table A5) with two exceptions from ammonia spikes. The low recovery on July 27 in 2009 (37 percent) in a spiked environmental sample matrix occurred when the spiked contribution (0.027 mg/L) was small in comparison to the sample concentration of 1.26 mg/L. The high recovery on July 27 in 2009 (mean of 140 percent) was in low-level spiked blank water. However, the recoveries of ammonia from mid-level and high-level spiked blank water on that date were 105 and 99 percent, respectively.

Results of quality-control sampling and analyses show improvement in the quality of data collected in 2010. Only one blank sample (5 percent of all blanks) for total nitrogen and one blank sample for ammonia, in 2010, contained a concentration larger than the MRL. The concentrations of these samples were 0.076 mg/L for total nitrogen and 0.017 mg/L for ammonia (the MRL for total nitrogen was 0.060 mg/L and the MRL for ammonia was 0.012 mg/L; appendix A, table A6). Concentrations in split and replicate samples for analytes common to both years were generally more variable in 2010 than in 2009, but the maximum mean difference in 2010 split samples was 15 percent (total phosphorus samples), and replicate samples in 2010 showed mean differences of 19 percent (for total phosphorus samples) or less, indicating that the data were of good quality (appendix A, tables A7 and A8). The sole exception to this was the phaeophytin a replicate samples, which had a mean relative difference of 27 percent. Phaeophtyin a is analyzed in the same samples collected and analyzed for chlorophyll a, and the mean relative difference in chlorophyll a samples was 16 percent, which is similar to the variation measured in most years. The coefficient of variation for interlaboratory split samples in 2010 was 30 percent (for nitrite plus nitrate and phaeophytin a on September 20, 2010) or less (appendix A, table A9), and there was little difference in the results of interlaboratory split events that year. In contrast to 2009 samples, ammonia interlaboratory split samples collected in 2010 and sent to the same laboratories as in 2009 showed a maximum coefficient of variation at 10 percent. Mean nutrient spike recoveries in 2010 ranged between 78 and 135 percent (appendix A, table A10) with two exceptions from total nitrogen spikes. The low-level spiked blank water on August 17 in 2010 had a recovery of 156 percent, but the recoveries of total nitrogen from mid-level and high-level spiked blank water on that date were 98 and 100 percent, respectively. The spiked environmental sample matrix on September 27 in 2010 had a high mean recovery of 157 percent (appendix A, table A10).

Results

Field crews collected data from a network of multiparameter continuous water-quality monitors, water-quality samples, and meteorological sites in Upper Klamath and Agency Lakes in 2009–10 to assess water-quality conditions and processes. The network provided data at high temporal resolutions that can be related to bloom conditions, weather, bathymetry, and currents and that are central to future water-quality modeling efforts. Continued operation of the monitoring sites and meteorological sites will provide a long-term dataset that will enable the identification of water-quality dynamics and trends in Upper Klamath Lake.

Water-Quality Monitors

In 2009, the lakewide daily median values calculated from Upper Klamath Lake continuous monitor data showed periods of extreme dissolved oxygen conditions (both super- and undersaturated) and pH (> 9) indicative of respiration (oxygenic photosynthesis) and subsequent decomposition during the AFA-dominated bloom cycle (fig. 2). Lakewide median dissolved oxygen concentrations (8–10 mg/L) and percent saturation (100–120 percent) were high at the beginning of the 2009 field season (early May) and declined in late June. The decline in dissolved oxygen conditions reached a minimum (3.3 mg/L, 44 percent) in late July coincident with a minimum in lakewide median pH (7.4) and elevated specific conductance (123 µS/cm; the seasonal maximum in specific conductance occurred several days later). These conditions were associated with the first rapid decline in the AFA-dominated bloom and are consistent with observations made in 2005, 2006, and 2008 (Hoilman and others, 2008; Lindenberg and others, 2009; Kannarr and others, 2010). A second period of elevated lakewide median pH (> 9) occurred between early August and late September, indicating a second period of elevated phytoplankton growth (fig. 2). Dissolved oxygen

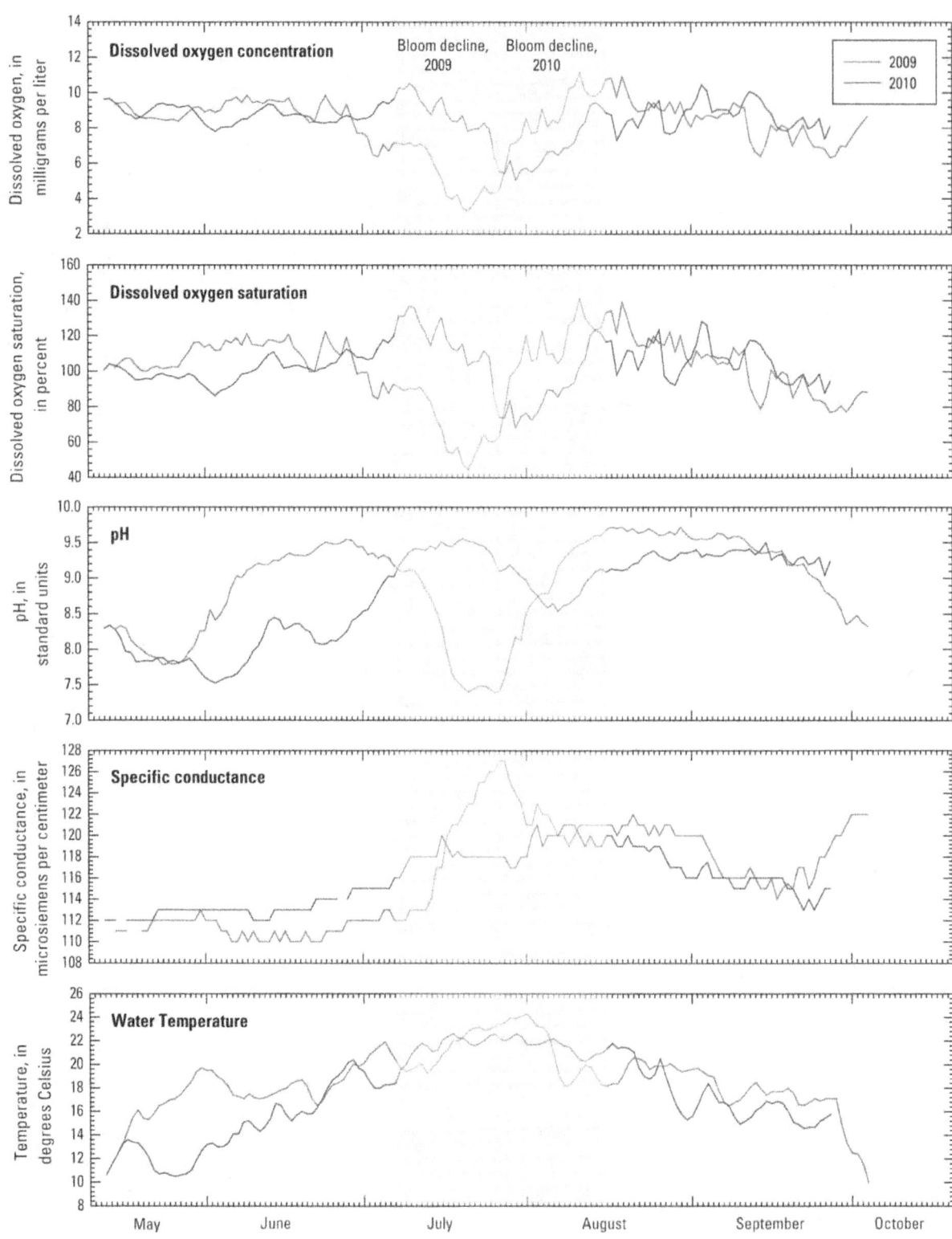

Figure 2. Graphs showing lakewide daily median dissolved oxygen concentration, dissolved oxygen percent saturation, pH, specific conductance, and water temperature in Upper Klamath Lake, Oregon, 2009–10. Data from nine open-water sites where continuous monitors were deployed were combined to calculate daily median values.

concentrations and pH values increased rapidly after the minima in late July, peaking in mid-August with values of 11.5 mg/L and 9.7 pH units respectively, and gradually declined to 8.6 mg/L and 8.3 pH units, respectively, on October 4 in 2009, the last day of data for the season. Dissolved oxygen saturation also followed these trends, decreasing to values below 100 percent after the first week in September, a pattern that continued into late September. These data are characteristic of two distinct AFA-dominated growth and decline events in the 2009 field season.

Two periods of elevated pH values (> 9.0) and dissolved oxygen conditions, representing AFA-dominated bloom growth, were also observed in 2010 (fig. 2). The first period occurred from early July to the beginning of August, and the second occurred from mid-August to late September. The pH maximum during the first period of elevation in 2010 occurred later in the season than during the first period of 2009. In 2010, the minimum lakewide daily median dissolved oxygen concentration and percent saturation, indicating a decline in the bloom, was less extreme (5.0 mg/L, 74 percent saturation) and occurred later in the season (on July 30, 2010) than in 2009. This minimum was nearly coincident with a pH minimum (8.5 pH units on August 7, 2010) and a peak in specific conductance (121 µS/cm on August 9, 2010). Following the pH and dissolved oxygen minima in late July–early August 2010, values gradually increased and remained steady for the rest of the season with pH values between 8.5 and 9.5 and dissolved oxygen concentrations between 5.5 and 10.5 mg/L (between 75 and 128 percent saturation). These data, along with the trends in chlorophyll *a* concentration (discussed below), show that the first and largest AFA-dominated growth and decline event of 2010 occurred later in the season than in 2009.

Lakewide daily median water temperatures in 2009 were greater in May and early June than in 2010 (fig. 2). The largest difference in water temperature between the two years occurred on May 29, when water temperature was 7.8°C warmer in 2009 than in 2010. In general, daily median water temperatures continued to be lower throughout the 2010 field season than in 2009. Daily median water temperatures peaked on August 1 in 2009 at 24.3°C and on July 30 in 2010 at 22.6°C. Water temperatures declined following these peaks in both years, although the initial decline after the peak was rapid over the first week in August 2009 and more gradual over the rest of the season in 2010.

In 2009 and 2010, water-quality conditions were also monitored at the Agency Lake northern and southern sites (AGN and AGS, respectively). Water-quality trends and the timing of minima in pH and dissolved oxygen concentrations at AGS in 2009 were similar to those in Upper Klamath Lake, whereas trends and timing between Upper Klamath Lake and AGN were different. For example, the AGN data do not show the late July minimum in pH that was observed at AGS (fig. 3) and in the Upper Klamath Lake lakewide pH median. A maximum in specific conductance occurred at AGS in late July, 2009, coincident with the maximum in Upper Klamath Lake, but unlike Upper Klamath Lake, a second maximum occurred in mid-August, nearly one month later.

As in Upper Klamath Lake, the 2010 dissolved oxygen conditions in Agency Lake were low to moderate compared to those in 2009. At AGS, for example, dissolved oxygen in 2010 varied little through the first half of June and ranged from a high of 210 percent saturation (15.9 mg/L) to a low of 47 percent (4.16 mg/L; fig. 4). pH values at AGS, after reaching a peak of 10 in mid-July 2010, remained at 9.6 or above through August, whereas in 2009, pH ranged between 10 and 7.3 over the same time period. Therefore, as in Upper Klamath Lake, there was evidence in Agency Lake that the AFA-dominated bloom cycle of growth and decline was weaker in 2010 than in 2009.

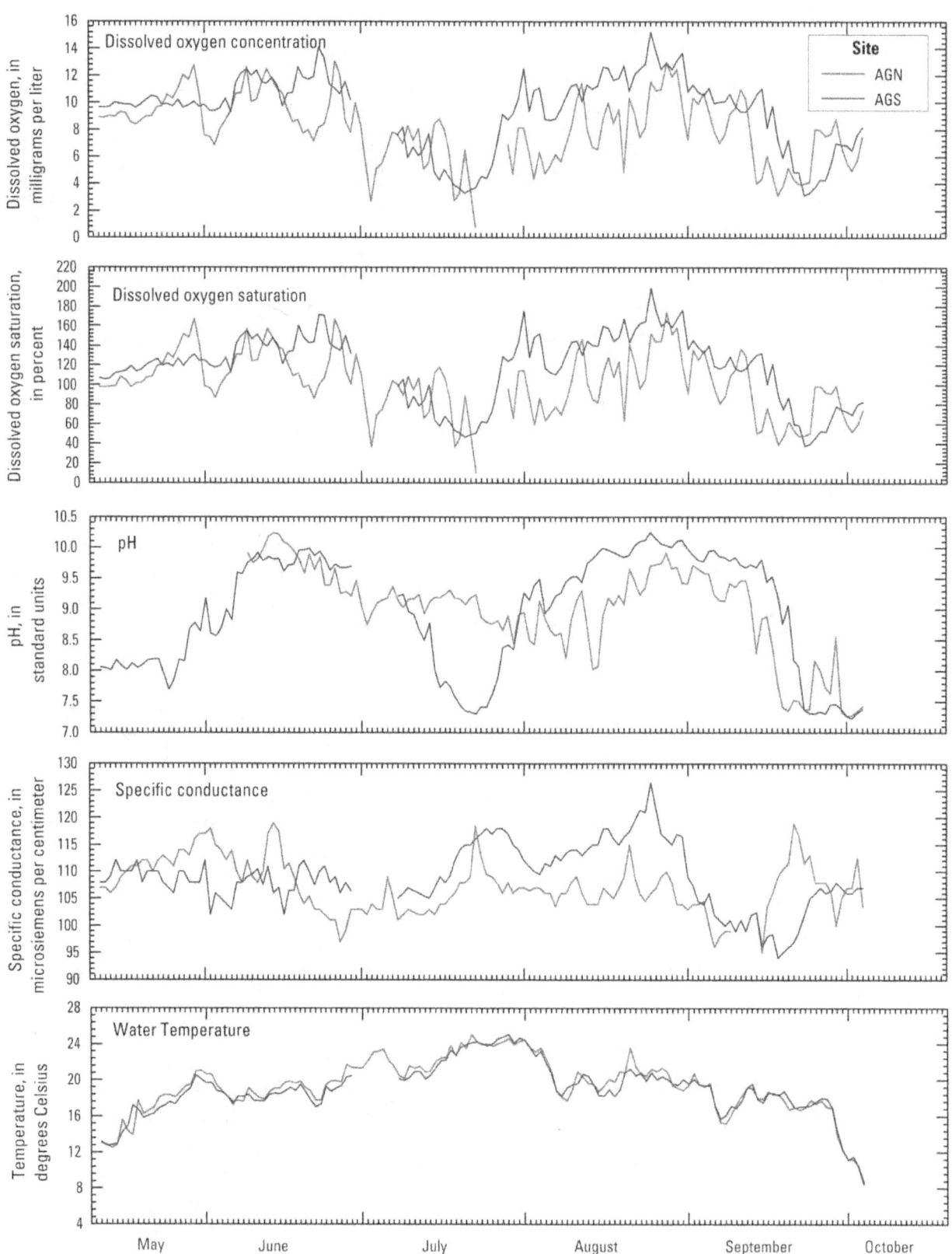

Figure 3. Graphs showing dissolved oxygen concentration, dissolved oxygen percent saturation, pH, specific conductance, and temperature in Agency Lake, Oregon, 2009.

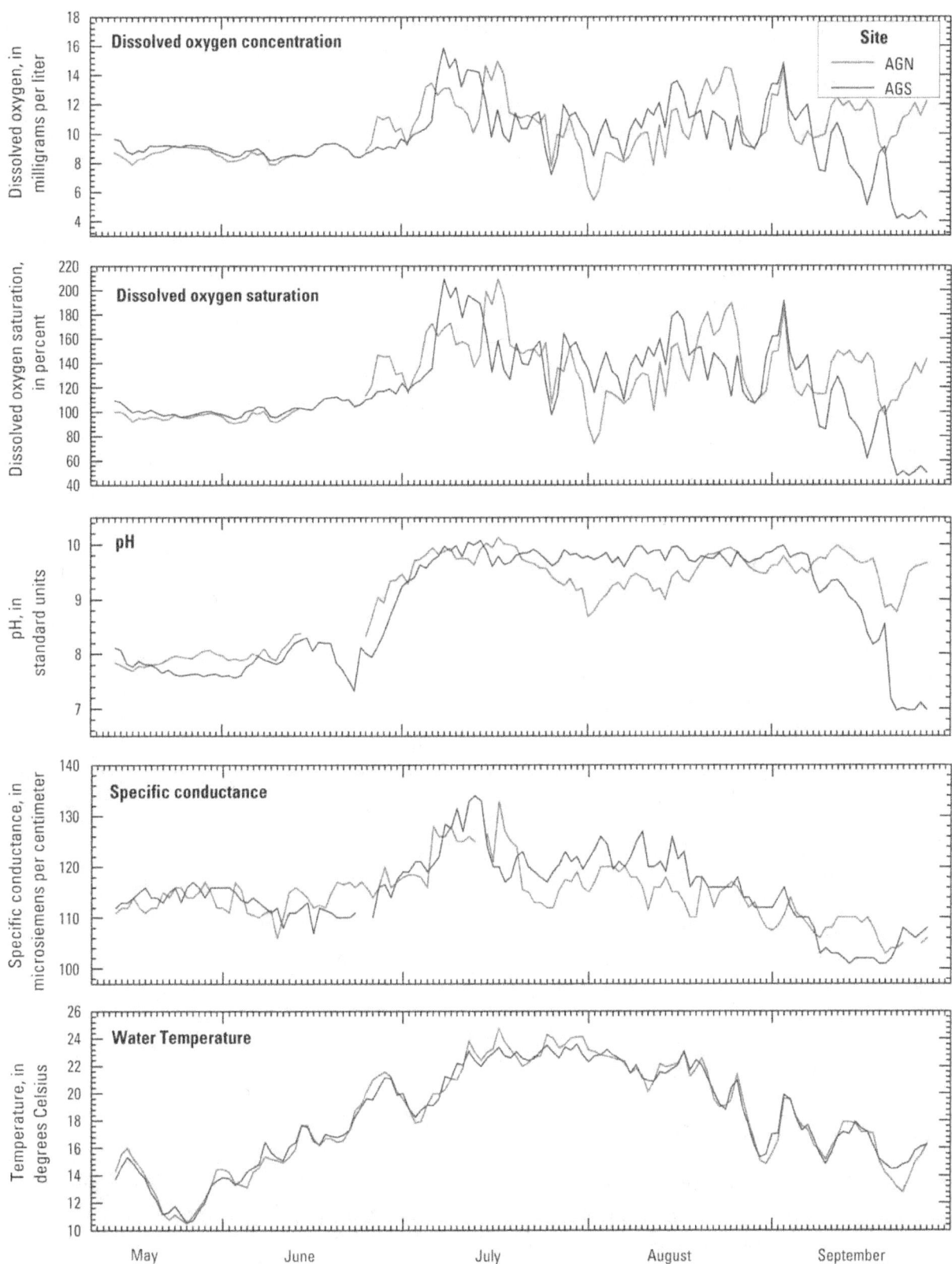

Figure 4. Graphs showing dissolved oxygen concentration, dissolved oxygen percent saturation, pH, specific conductance, and temperature in Agency Lake, Oregon, 2010.

Water-Quality Samples

In 2009, peak concentrations of chlorophyll *a* occurred at several sites in late June, and again in late August through early September (fig. 5), indicating two distinct growth periods of the AFA-dominated bloom that year. The early season peak values of chlorophyll *a* occurred on June 30 in 2009 at RPT, MDT, EPT, and MDN and at concentrations of 419, 281, 149, and 162 µg/L, respectively. Concentrations peaked again at these sites between August 17 and September 14 in 2009, with concentrations of 157, 314, 143, and 317 µg/L, respectively. Two distinct highs were also observed in samples from WMR, although concentrations were generally lower at this site. Chlorophyll *a* concentrations decreased over 3 to 5 weeks after both peaks in 2009, coincident with decreases in dissolved oxygen concentration and pH, indicating a period of bloom decline and associated phytoplankton degradation. Total phosphorus and total nitrogen concentrations also peaked at several sites in late June to early July and again in mid-August to early September, following the trends in chlorophyll *a* at each site and reflecting the incorporation of nitrogen and phosphorus into biomass (fig. 5). In general, total phosphorus and total nitrogen concentrations increased throughout the sample season without decreasing during the major bloom decline periods. This indicates that much of the phosphorus and nitrogen measured as total concentrations during periods of bloom decline were in the form of dissolved nutrients, which are released as cells lyse and decompose. Concentrations of dissolved nutrients (orthophosphate, ammonia, and nitrite plus nitrate) remained low through June and most of July and increased at all sites during the first decline in chlorophyll *a* concentrations. Maximum concentrations of un-ionized ammonia occurred in late August–early September 2009, after the maxima in total ammonia concentrations and during the second period of elevated pH following the major bloom decline (appendix C, table C1). Concentrations remained below 260 µg/L, well below the level determined by Saiki

and others (1999) to be lethal for endangered larval and juvenile suckers. Nitrite plus nitrate concentrations were less than 100 µg/L at all sites for most of the 2009 field season, although there was a noticeable increase in late September at WMR and RPT, the two shallow sites.

In 2010, chlorophyll *a* concentrations remained at or near the detection limit until early July. Concentrations at all sites increased in July, and there was evidence of a weak decline between mid-July and the beginning of August at all sites except MDT. After that, chlorophyll *a* concentrations at all sites increased to seasonal maximum values in late August or in September. The early season peak values were generally lower and occurred nearly three weeks later than in 2009. Chlorophyll a concentrations measured on July 19 were 59, 59, 89, and < 292 µg/L at MDN, WMR, EPT, and MDT, respectively. Overall, the decline of the bloom between July 19 and August 2 in 2010 started from lower peak values and was weaker than the bloom decline between June 30 and July 21 in 2009. The 2010 decline was not apparent at all of the sites visited. At MDT, chlorophyll *a* concentrations were 252 µg/L on August 2, while concentrations at the other three sites visited were between 4.6 and 26.2 µg/L. In 2010, total phosphorus and total nitrogen concentrations largely followed the trends in chlorophyll *a* at each site and, compared to 2009, remained at lower values well into July (fig. 6). However, the seasonal maximum values were higher for total phosphorus at MDN, WMR, EPT, and MDT, respectively, in 2010 (260, 340, 310, and 800 µg/L) than in 2009 (290, 250, 240 and 390 µg/L).

Peak concentrations of orthophosphate, ammonia, and nitrite plus nitrate occurred between late July and early August in 2010 with the first minor bloom decline. These peaks were followed by decreasing concentrations through the first half of September and increasing concentrations to smaller maxima in late September. Dissolved nutrient concentrations were also lower in 2010 than in 2009.

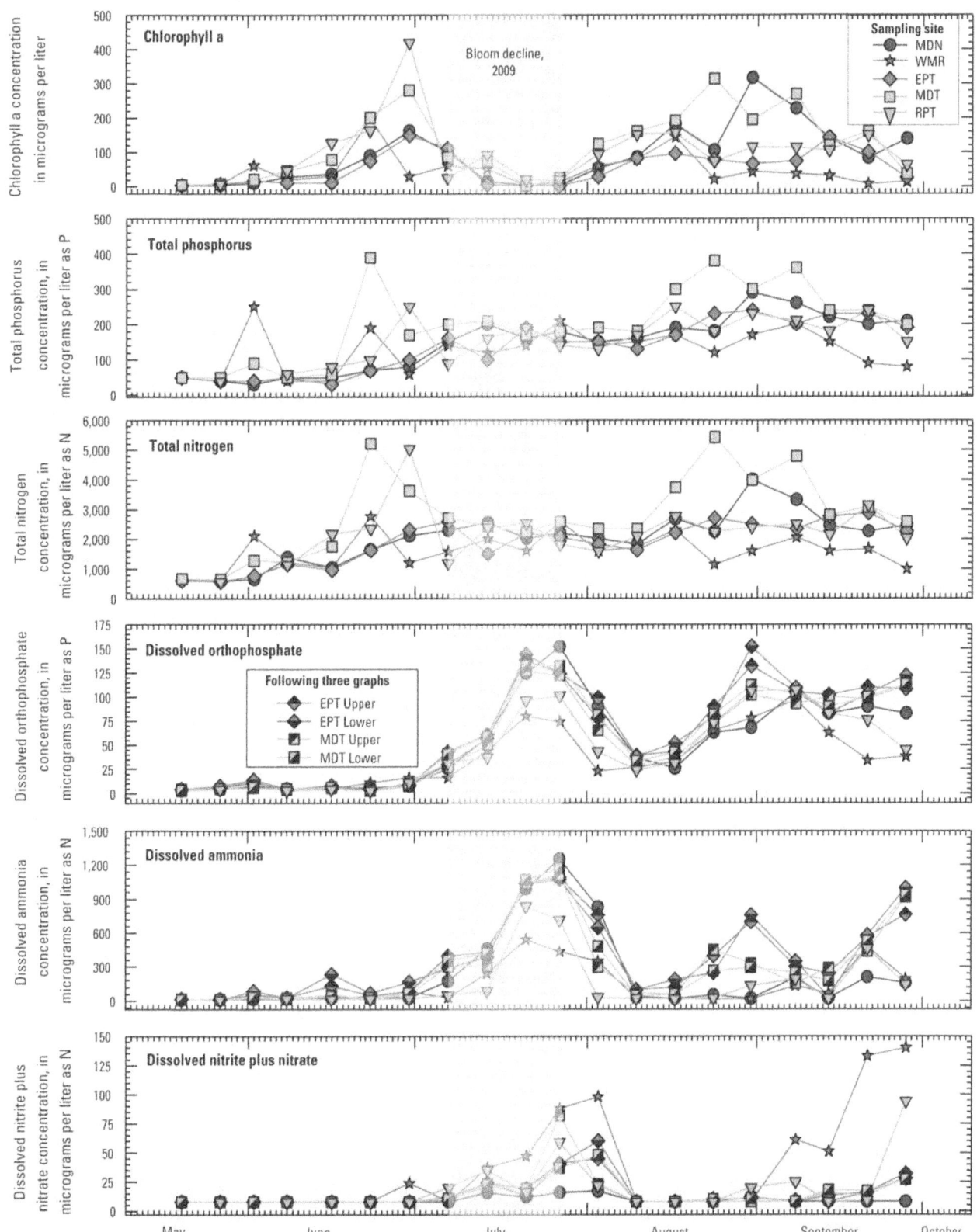

Figure 5. Graphs showing concentrations of chlorophyll *a*, total phosphorus, total nitrogen, orthophosphate, ammonia, and nitrite plus nitrate, Upper Klamath Lake, Oregon, 2009. Site descriptions are shown in table 2.

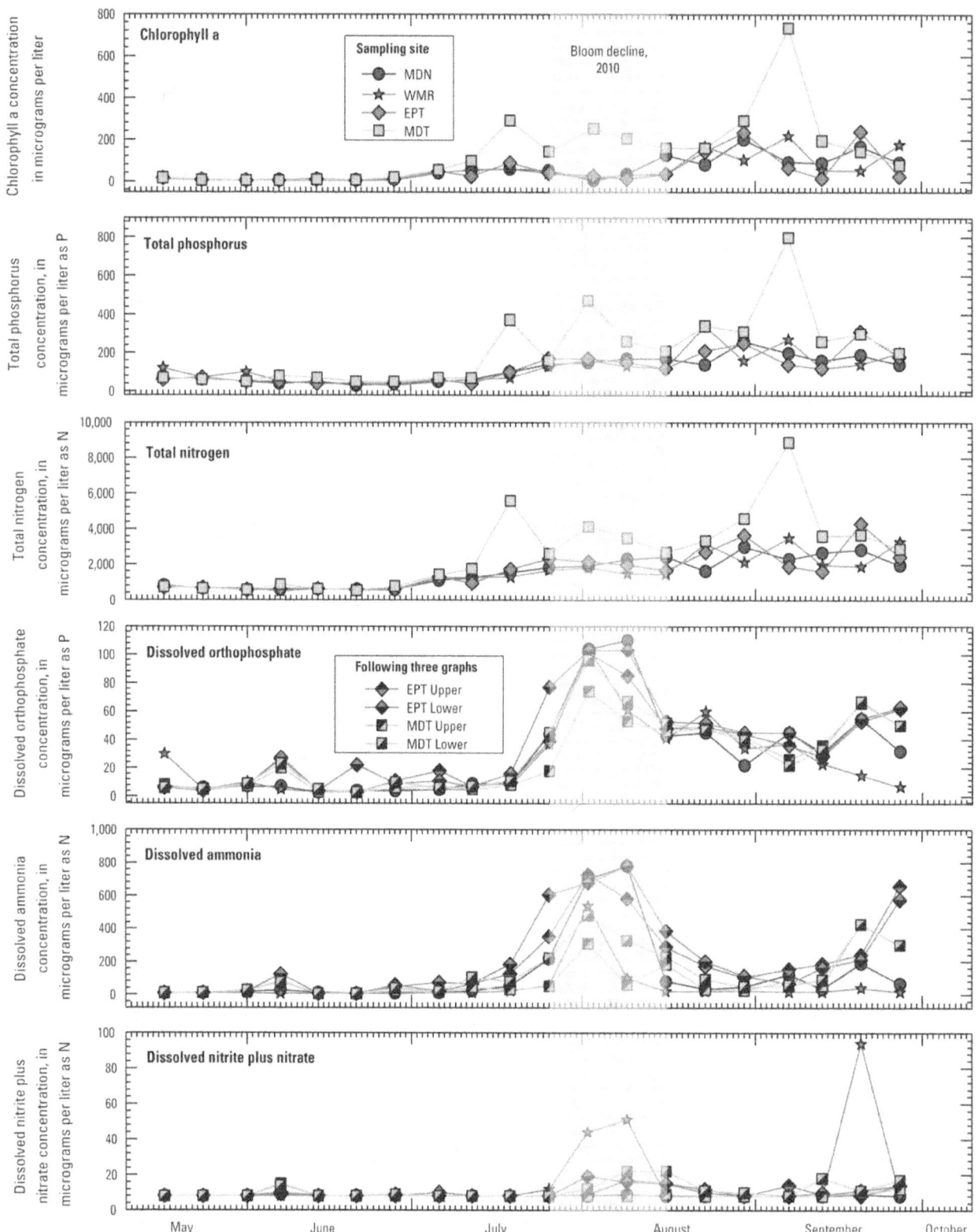

Figure 6. Graphs showing concentrations of chlorophyll *a*, total phosphorus, total nitrogen, orthophosphate, ammonia, and nitrite plus nitrate, Upper Klamath Lake, Oregon, 2010. Site descriptions are shown in table 2.

Peak values of 110 µg/L orthophosphate, 779 µg/L ammonia, and 94 µg/L nitrite plus nitrate were measured at MDN in 2010, while peak values of 152 µg/L orthophosphate, 1,250 µg/L ammonia, and 170 µg/L nitrite plus nitrate were recorded at MDN in 2009. Overall, changes in 2010 dissolved nutrient concentrations were similar to those observed in 2009, but the range of values was less pronounced. This pattern was also delayed by several weeks in 2010 compared to 2009. Maximum concentrations of un-ionized ammonia were observed at most sites in mid-July to early August in 2010, temporally overlapping more than in 2009 with the seasonal ammonia concentration maxima (appendix C, table C2). Differences in nutrient dynamics observed between 2009 and 2010 show that, although seasonal water-quality conditions on Upper Klamath Lake are highly variable, some patterns are consistently observed from year to year.

Total particulate nitrogen, phosphorus, and carbon concentrations were measured in water samples collected in 2009 only (fig. 7). Peak concentrations were observed at most sites in late June, corresponding with peaks in chlorophyll a (figs. 5 and 7). Maximum concentrations of particulate carbon and nutrients occurred at RPT on June 30, 2009, with concentrations of 4.76 mg/L particulate nitrogen, 0.26 mg/L particulate phosphorus, and 23.8 mg/L particulate carbon. Particulate carbon and nutrient concentrations at all sites decreased after the first peak in late June to minimum values in mid-July that coincided with the bloom decline (as determined by chlorophyll a concentrations and maxima in dissolved nutrient concentrations). From mid-July to the end of August, concentrations of particulate nutrients generally followed the same trends as chlorophyll a and total nitrogen and phosphorus concentrations.

Particulate carbon to particulate phosphorus ratios (C:P) and particulate nitrogen to particulate phosphorus ratios (N:P) were calculated using particulate nutrient data from 2009 (figs. 8 and 9). Median values of both C:P and N:P ratios were highest (exceeding 100 and 20, respectively) from June 16 to June 23. This was the period of most rapid growth in the bloom. After June 23, both ratios decreased, and biweekly medians remained below 100 and 20, respectively, through August 31, although both ratios exhibited significant variability between sites on any given sampling day. Lowest median values occurred on July 27 in 2009 at 60.3 for C:P and on July 21 in 2009 at 8.00 for N:P (shown within the range of values between July 14 and July 21, 2009, when the median N:P ratio was 12), coinciding with low chlorophyll a concentrations and elevated dissolved nutrient concentrations (fig. 5) at most sites.

Particulate inorganic carbon and phosphorus samples were collected at MDN and MDT (two samples were collected at MDT, at one-quarter and three-quarters of total water depth) during the 2009 field season. At MDN, nine samples were collected for particulate inorganic phosphorus from June 16, 2009, through August 31, 2009, and four samples were collected for particulate inorganic carbon from June 16, 2009, through July 7, 2009. Particulate inorganic carbon was not detected in any samples above the method detection limit of 0.076 mg/L and, as a fraction of the total particulate carbon, never exceeded 0.026 mg/L in all samples. Particulate inorganic phosphorus was measured in nine samples from MDN (concentrations between 0.007 and 0.069 mg/L) and in five samples each from MDT at one-quarter and three-quarters water column depths (concentrations between 0.012 and 0.068 at one-quarter depth and between 0.013 and 0.090 mg/L at three-quarters depth; fig. 7). As a fraction of the total particulate phosphorus, particulate inorganic phosphorus ranged from 0.25 on June 16, 2011, to 0.79 on August 17, 2009.

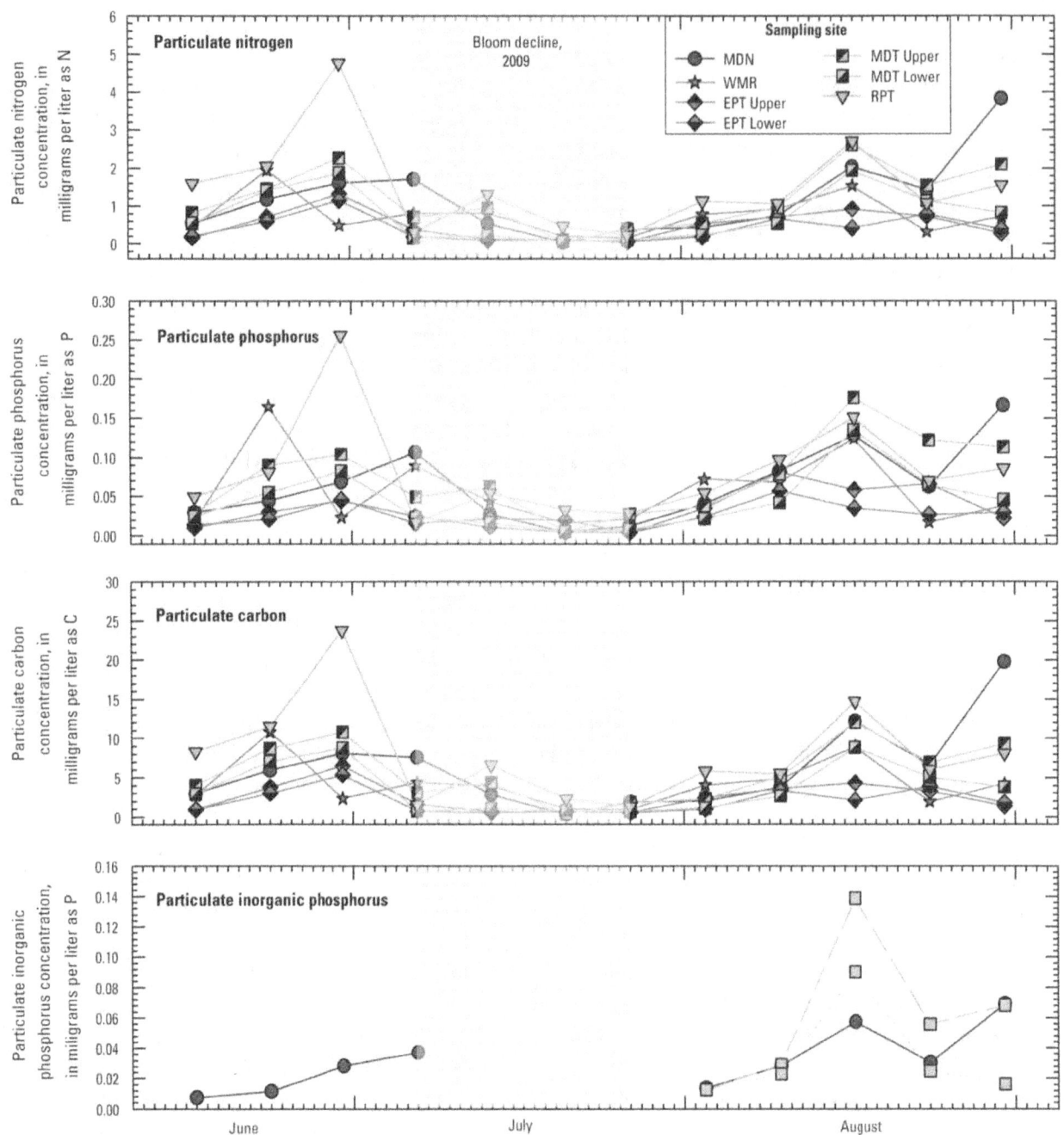

Figure 7. Graphs showing concentrations of particulate nitrogen, particulate phosphorus, particulate carbon, and particulate inorganic phosphourus, Upper Klamath Lake, Oregon, 2009. Site descriptions are shown in table 2.

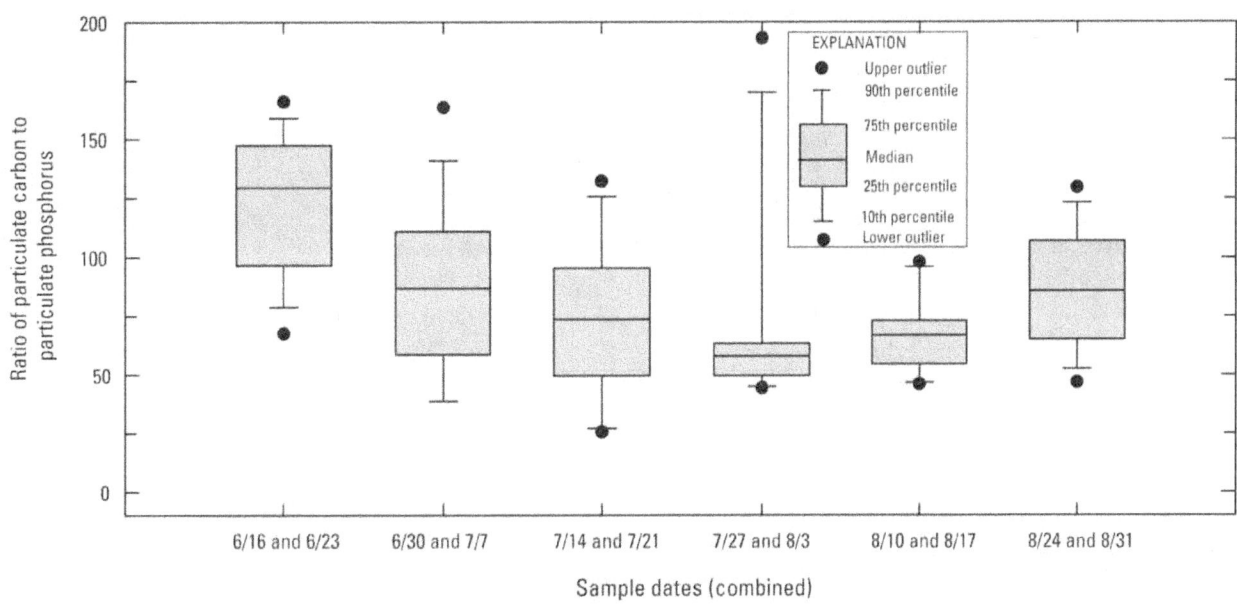

Figure 8. Box and whisker graph showing lakewide ratios for particulate carbon to particulate phosphorus (C:P), Upper Klamath Lake, Oregon, 2009. Data from two consecutive sample weeks are grouped in each box and whisker plot (N=14).

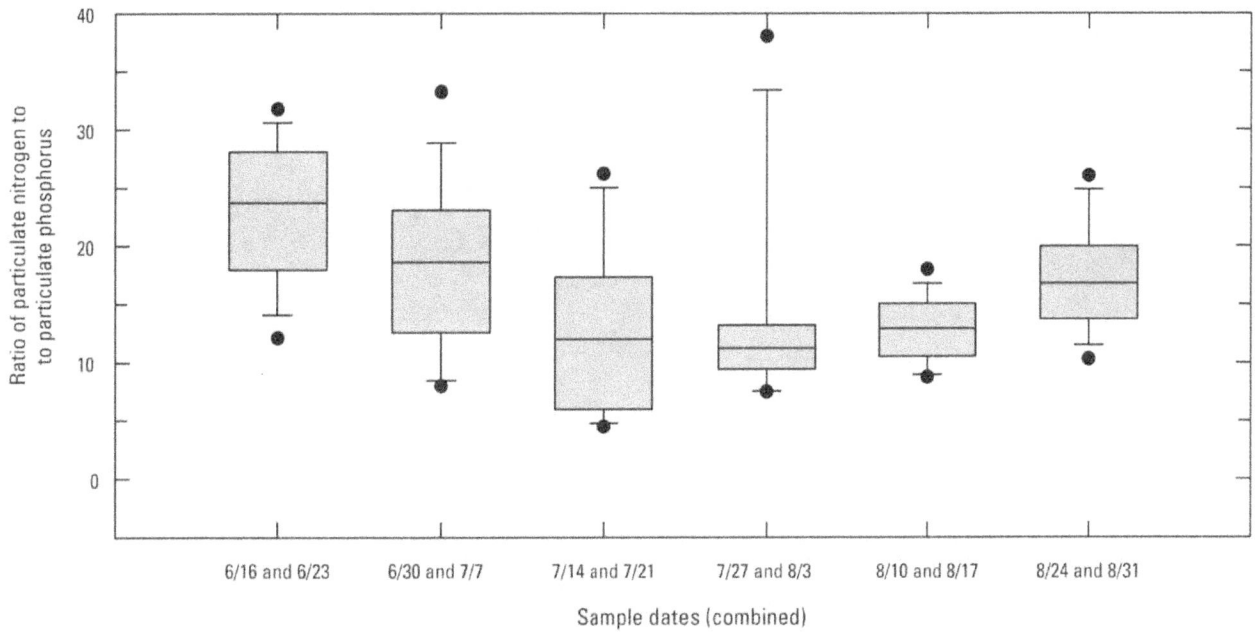

Figure 9. Box and whisker graph showing lakewide ratios for particulate nitrogen to particulate phosphorus (N:P), Upper Klamath Lake, Oregon, 2009. Data from two consecutive sample weeks are grouped in each box and whisker plot (N=14). See figure 8 for explanation of plot components.

Meteorological Data

Box and whisker graphs were constructed using the daily median values from WRW-MET (fig. 1, table 2) in 2009 and 2010 (fig. 10). Between June and September, 2009 and 2010, daily median wind speeds were widely variable but typically between 1 and 6 m/s (fig. 10A). Wind speeds were higher and more variable in June and July 2010 than during the same period in 2009. The maximum daily median wind speed was 5.5 m/s in 2009 and 6.2 m/s in 2010. The June 2009 interquartile range for daily median wind speed was 2.3–3.1 m/s, whereas the June 2010 interquartile range was 2.0–4.2 m/s. Wind direction data collected between October 1 in 2008 and September 30 in 2010 show that the highest winds were predominantly from the west at sites MDN and WRW (figs. 11 and 12), which are at the northern end of Upper Klamath Lake.

The meteorological sites located on the southern end of the lake and shoreline, HDB, MDL, and SSHR, recorded highest winds predominantly from the north-northwest. Winds recorded at BLB were predominantly from the north to northwest, and a second prevailing wind occurred from the south.

The daytime solar radiation median values (fig. 10A) reflect patterns of clear sunny days typical in the Klamath Basin during the summer season. Higher median values of solar radiation occurred in June 2009 than in the same month in 2010, indicating more partly cloudy days in June 2010. Median values for August and September were similar for both years. Following the peak of each year, maximum solar radiation values gradually began to decline with the shorter days of the fall and winter.

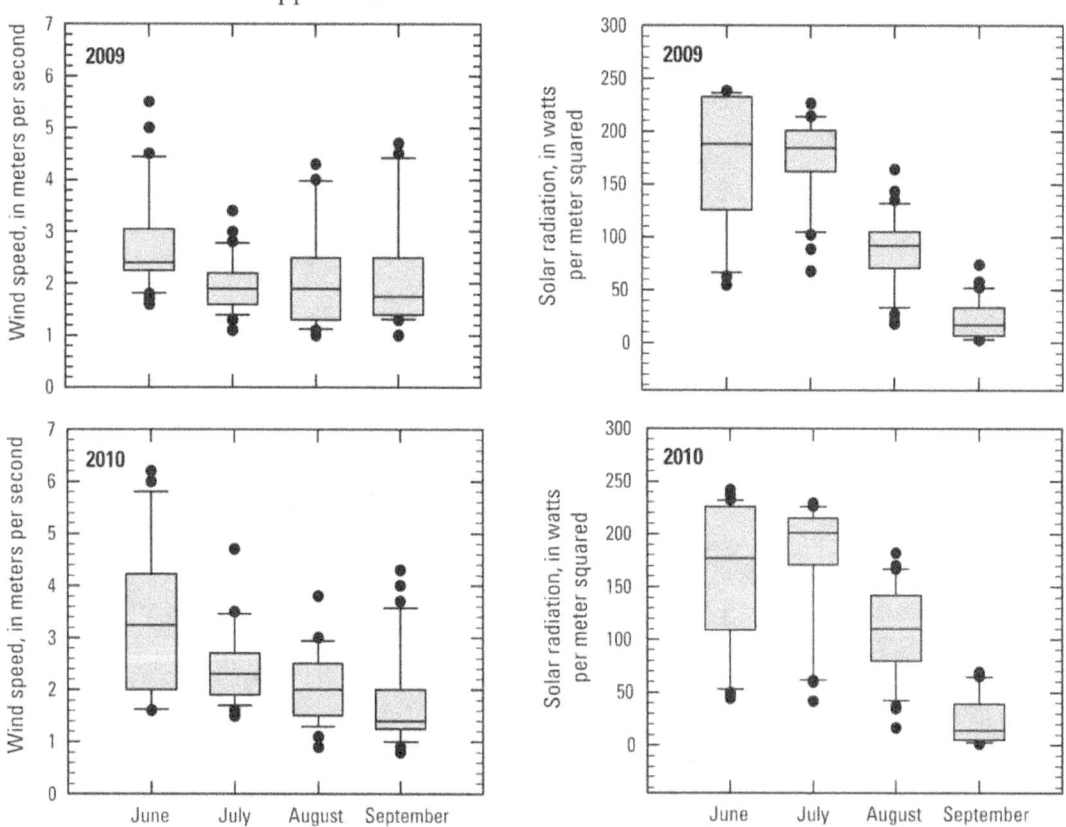

Figure 10A. Box and whisker graphs showing daily median wind speed and solar radiation at WRW meteorological site from June through September, Upper Klamath Lake, Oregon, 2009–10. See figure 8 for explanation of plot components.

Air temperature was higher in June 2009 (median value 14.7°C) than in June 2010 (median value 13.5°C) (fig. 10B). Air temperatures peaked in July of both years, but were higher in 2009 (median value 22.1°C) than in 2010 (median value 21.1°C). Overall, air temperatures in June, July, and September were higher in 2009 than in 2010, and in August they were similar (median values of 18.8°C and 19.1°C in 2009 and 2010, respectively).

Relative humidity was higher in June 2009 (median 71 percent) than in June 2010 (median 64 percent)(fig. 10B). However, in September, the median relative humidity was 72 percent in 2010, compared to 58 percent in 2009. Median relative humidity values were nearly equal and the lowest of the season during July and August of both years. Minimum values of relative humidity typically correlated with peak values in air temperature, illustrating the Klamath Basin's semiarid climate.

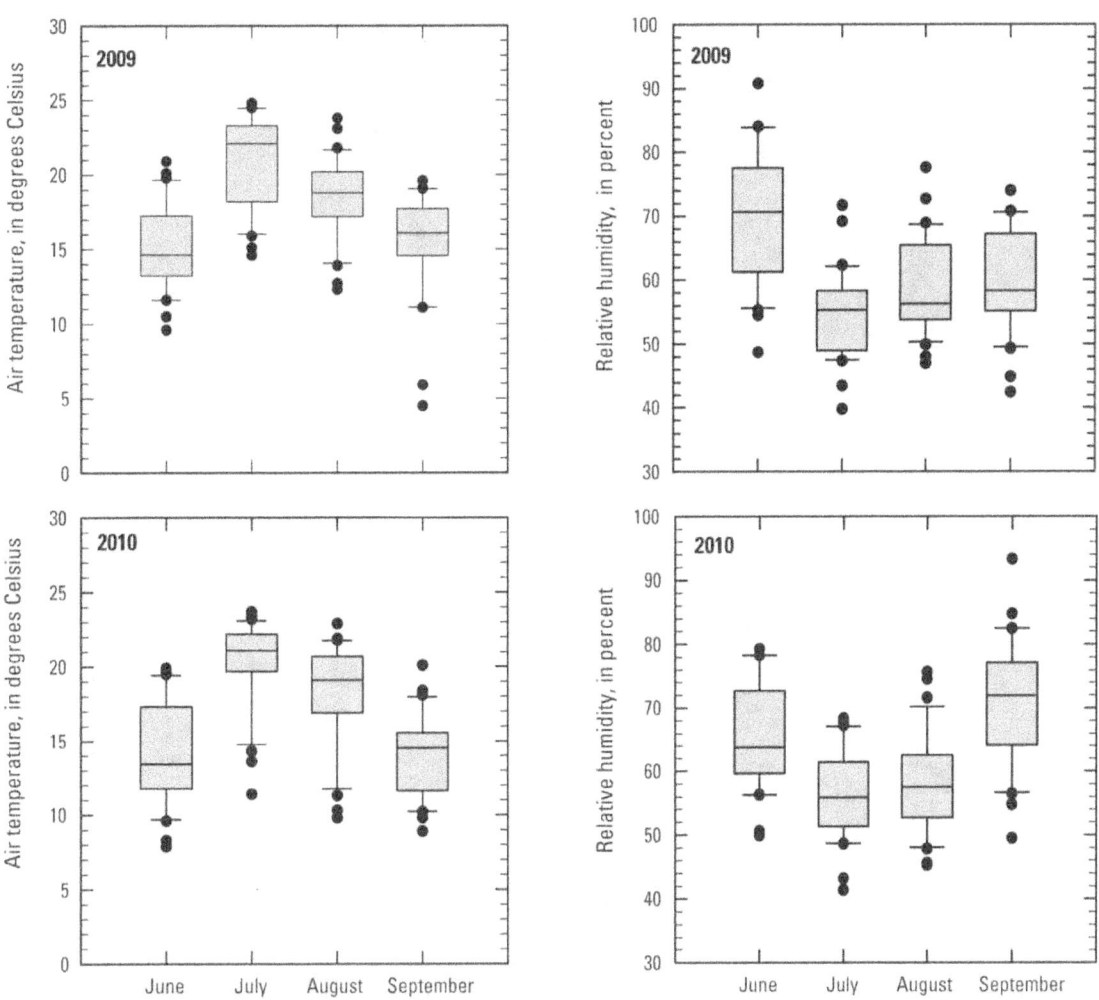

Figure 10B. Box and whisker graphs showing daily median wind air temperature and relative humidity at WRW meteorological site from June through September, Upper Klamath Lake, Oregon, 2009–10. See figure 8 for explanation of plot components.

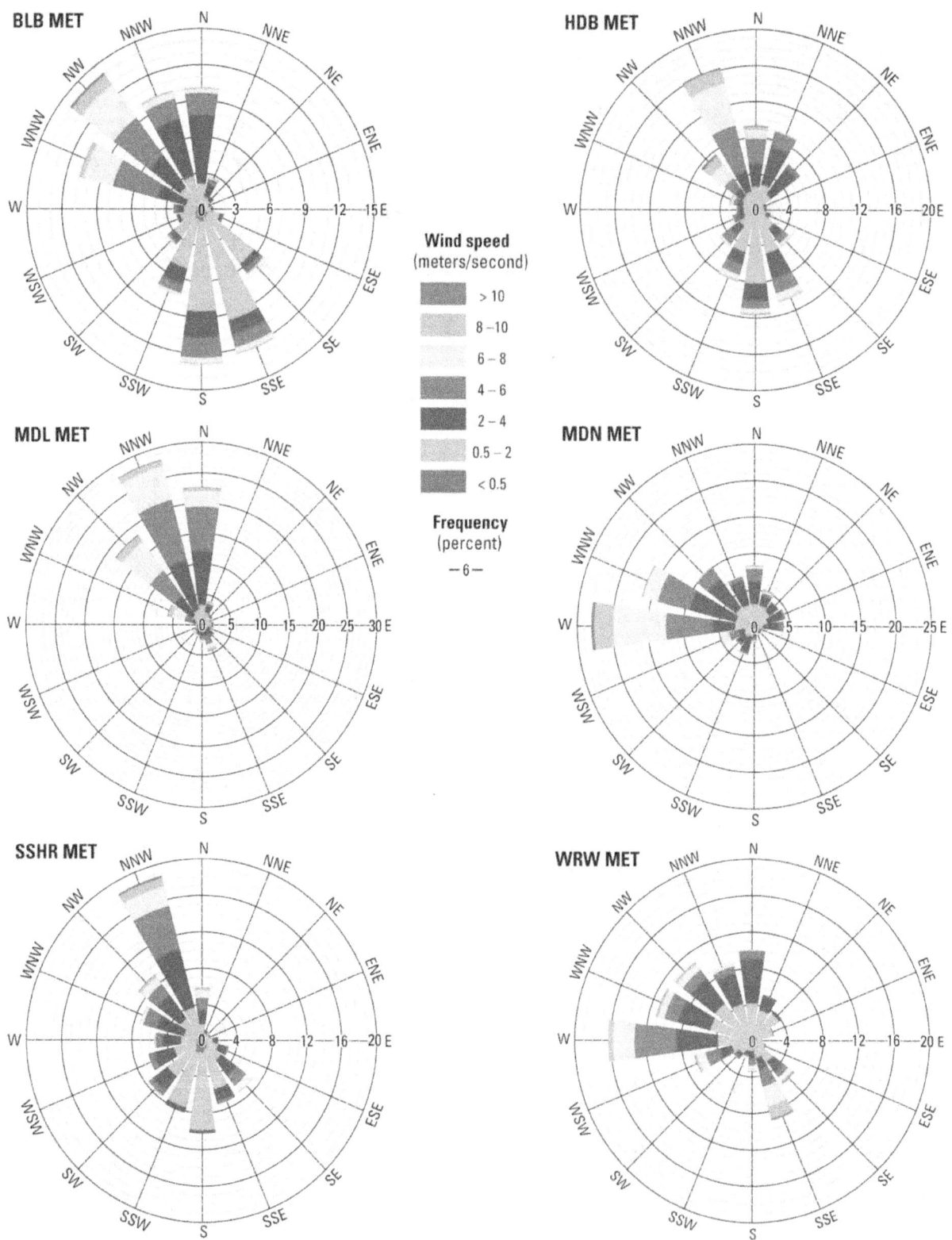

Figure 11. Histograms showing wind speed and direction for meteorological (MET) sites near Upper Klamath Lake, Oregon, 2009. Site descriptions are shown in table 3.

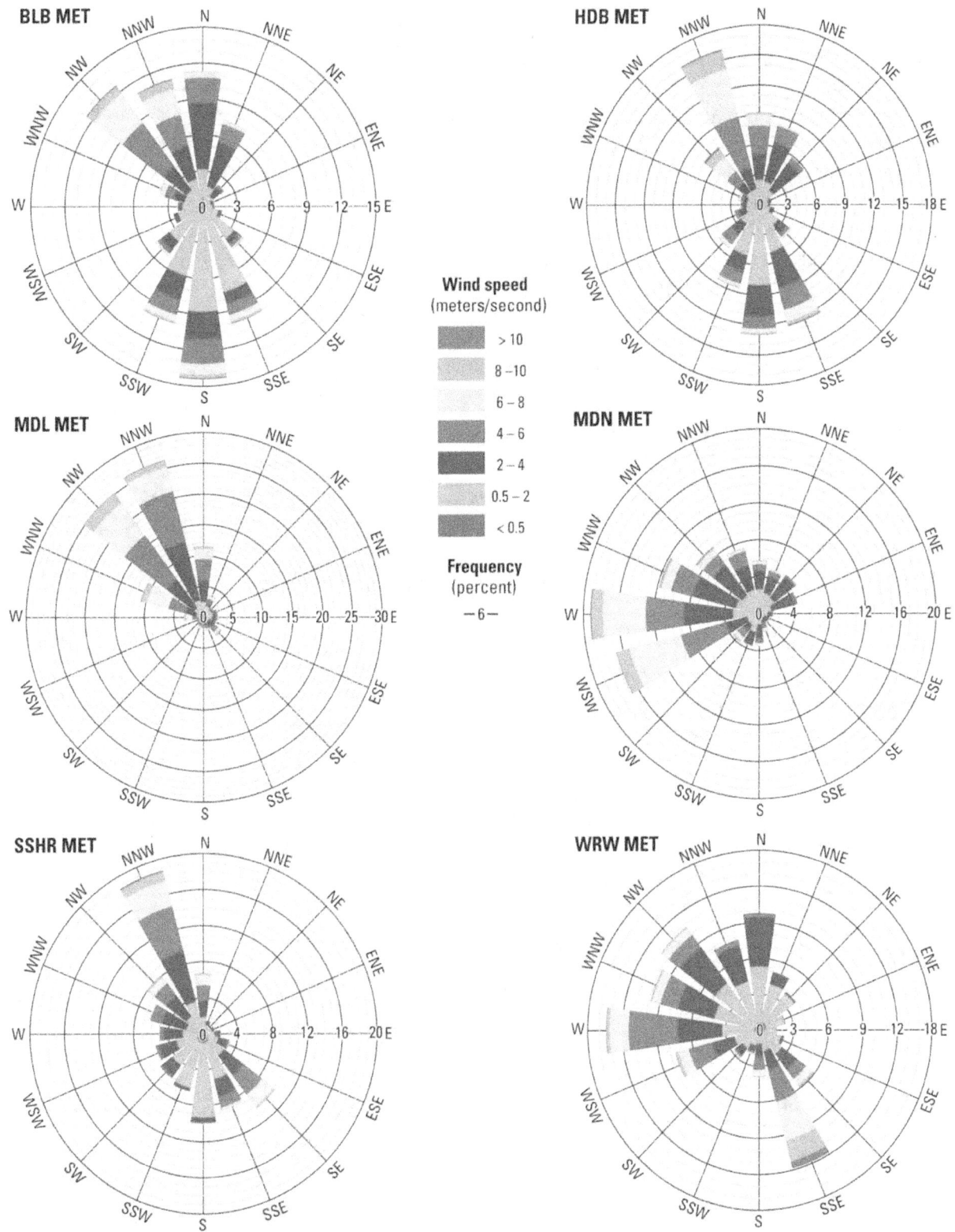

Figure 12. Histograms showing wind speed and direction for meteorological (MET) sites near Upper Klamath Lake, Oregon, 2010. Site descriptions are shown in table 3.

The meteorological data generally show that 2009 was less windy and more humid early in the season, had more clear days in June, and was warmer throughout the summer and early fall than during the same time periods in 2010. These differences in weather may help to account for the larger early bloom and more severe bloom decline observed in 2009, which has been previously cited (Perkins and others, 2000; Kann and Welch, 2005). In years when a severe midseason bloom decline has been observed on Upper Klamath Lake, the decline has often occurred during periods of sustained high temperature and low wind (Wood and others, 2006; Hoilman and others, 2008; Lindenberg and others, 2009; Kannarr and others, 2010), which increases water column stability (Kann and Welch, 2005) and permits the development of dense phytoplankton blooms (Eldridge and others, 2012).

Acknowledgments

We thank the reviewers who provided comments on this document. We also gratefully acknowledge the assistance of Scott Vanderkooi and many personnel of the USGS Klamath Falls Field Station for facilitating the water-quality field program with the use of boats, trucks, field equipment, and office and laboratory facilities. Many people contributed to the field work of this study: Mary Lindenberg (2009), Kristofor Kannarr (2009 and 2010), Cynthia King (2009), Kristin Harbin (2009 and 2010), and Matthew Wilson (2009). The efforts of Amy Brooks and Matt Johnston from the USGS Oregon Water Science Center in processing and checking the continuous datasets were critical to the success of the monitoring program.

References Cited

American Public Health Association, 2005, Standard methods for the examination of water and wastewater (21st ed.): Washington, D.C., American Public Health Association, 1200 p.

Aspila, K.I., Agemian, Haig, and Chau, A.S.Y., 1976, A semi-automated method for the determination of inorganic, organic and total phosphate in sediments: Analyst, v. 101, p. 187–197.

Banish, N.P., Adams, B.J., Shively, R.S., Mazur, M.M., Beauchamp, D.A., and Wood, T.M., 2009, Distribution and habitat associations of radio-tagged adult Lost River and shortnose suckers in Upper Klamath Lake, Oregon: Bethesda, Maryland, Transactions of the American Fisheries Society, v. 138, p. 153–168.

Bureau of Reclamation, 2000, Klamath project—Historic operation: Klamath Falls, Oregon, Bureau of Reclamation, 53 p. plus appendixes. [Also available at *http://www.usbr.gov/mp/kbao/docs/Historic%2 0Operation.pdf*]

Eldridge, S.L.C., Wood, T.M., and Echols, K.R., 2012, Spatial and temporal dynamics of cyanotoxins and their relation to other water quality variables in Upper Klamath Lake, Oregon, 2007–2009: U.S. Geological Survey Scientific Investigations Report 2012-5069, 34 p. [Also available at *http://pubs.usgs.gov/sir/2012/5069/.*]

Fishman, M.J., ed., 1993, Methods of analysis by the U.S. Geological Survey National Water Quality Laboratory; determination of inorganic and organic constituents in water and fluvial sediments: U.S. Geological Survey Open-File Report 93–125, 217 p.

Hoilman, G.R., Lindenberg, M.K., and Wood, T.M., 2008, Water quality conditions in Upper Klamath and Agency Lakes, Oregon, 2005: U.S. Geological Survey Scientific Investigations Report 2008–5026, 44 p. [Also available at *http://pubs.usgs.gov/sir/2008/5026/.*]

Hubbard, L.L., 1970, Water budget of Upper Klamath Lake, southwestern Oregon: U.S. Geological Survey Hydrologic Atlas 351, 1 plate.

Janney, E.C., Shively, R.S., Hayes, B.S., Barry, P.M., Perkins, D., 2008, Demographic analysis of Lost River Sucker and Shortnose Sucker populations in Upper Klamath Lake, Oregon: Transactions of the American Fisheries Society, v. 137, p 1812–1825.

Johnson, D.M., 1985, Atlas of Oregon lakes: Corvallis, Oregon State University Press, 317 p.

Kann, J., 1997, Ecology and water quality dynamics of a shallow hypereutrophic lake dominated by cyanobacteria (*Aphanizomenon flos-aquae*): Chapel Hill, University of North Carolina, Master's thesis, 110 p.

Kann, J., and Welch, E.B., 2005, Wind control on water quality in shallow, hypereutrophic Upper Klamath Lake, Oregon: Lake and Reservoir Management, v. 21, no. 2, p. 149–158.

Kannarr, K.E., Tanner, D.Q., Lindenberg, M.K., and Wood, T.M., 2010, Water-quality data from Upper Klamath and Agency Lakes, Oregon, 2007–08: U.S. Geological Survey Open-File Report 2010–1073, 28 p. [Also available at *http://pubs.usgs.gov/of/2010/1073/.*]

Lindenberg, M.K., Hoilman, Gene, and Wood, T.M., 2009, Water quality conditions in Upper Klamath and Agency Lakes, Oregon, 2006: U.S. Geological Survey Scientific Investigations Report 2008–5201, 54 p. [Also available at *http://pubs.usgs.gov/sir/2008/5201/.*]

Patton, C.J., and Kryskalla, J.R., 2003, Methods of analysis by the U.S. Geological Survey National Water Quality Laboratory— Evaluation of alkaline persulfate digestion as an alternative to Kjeldahl digestion for determination of total and dissolved nitrogen and phosphorus in water: U.S. Geological Survey Water-Resources Investigations Report 03–4174, 33 p.

Perkins, D., Kann, J., and Scoppettone, G.G., 2000, The role of poor water quality and fish kills in the decline of endangered Lost River and shortnose suckers in Upper Klamath Lake: U.S. Geological Survey, Biological Resources Division report submitted to Bureau of Reclamation, Klamath Falls Project Office, Klamath Falls, Oregon, Contract 4-AA-29-12160.

Saiki, M.K., Monda, D.P., and Bellerud, B.L., 1999, Lethal levels of selected water quality variables to larval and juvenile Lost River and shortnose suckers: Environmental Pollution, v. 105, p. 37–44.

Stubbs, K., and White, R., 1993, Lost River (*Deltistes luxatus*) and shortnose (*Chasmistes brevirostris*) sucker recovery plan: Portland, Oregon, U.S. Fish and Wildlife Service, 108 p.

U.S. Environmental Protection Agency, 1979a, Aqueous ammonia equilibrium—Tabulation of percent un-ionized ammonia: Duluth, Minnesota, EPA-600/3-79-091, 428 p.

U.S. Environmental Protection Agency, 1979b, Methods for chemical analysis of water and wastes: Cincinnati, Ohio, EPA-600/4-79-020, 460 p.

U.S. Geological Survey, 2006, Collection of water samples (ver. 2.0): U.S. Geological Survey Techniques of Water-Resources Investigations, book 9, chap. A4. [Also available at *http://pubs.water.usgs.gov/twri9A4/.*

U.S. Geological Survey, variously dated, National field manual for the collection of water-quality data: U.S. Geological Survey Techniques of Water-Resources Investigations, book 9, chaps. A1–A5 [Also available at *http://pubs.water.usgs.gov/twri9A/*]

Wagner, R.J., Boulger, R.W., Jr., Oblinger, C.J., and Smith, B.A., 2006, Guidelines and standard procedures for continuous water-quality monitors—Station operation, record computation, and data reporting: U.S. Geological Survey Techniques and Methods 1–D3, 51 p. plus attachments. [Also available at http://pubs.usgs.gov/tm/2006/tm1D3/]

Wong, S., Hendrixson, H., and Doehring, C., 2010, Post-restoration water quality conditions at the Williamson River Delta, Upper Klamath Basin, Oregon, 2007–2009: The Nature Conservancy, Klamath Falls, Oregon, 63 p. [Also available at http://conserveonline.org/library/post-restoration-water-quality-conditions-at-the/@@view.html]

Wood, T.M., Cheng, R.T., Gartner, J.W., Hoilman, G.R., Lindenberg, M.K., and Wellman, R.E., 2008, Modeling hydrodynamics and heat transport in Upper Klamath Lake, Oregon, and implications for water quality: U.S. Geological Survey Scientific Investigations Report 2008–5076, 48 p. [Also available at http://pubs.usgs.gov/sir/2008/5076/.]

Wood, T.M., Hoilman, G.R., and Lindenberg, M.K., 2006, Water quality conditions in Upper Klamath Lake, Oregon, 2002–2004: U.S. Geological Survey Scientific Investigations Report 2006–5209, 52 p. [Also available at http://pubs.usgs.gov/sir/2006/5209/.]

Zimmerman, C.F., Keefe, C.W., and Bashe, J., 1997, Method 440.0: Determination of carbon and nitrogen in sediments and particulates of estuarine/coastal waters using elemental analysis: National Exposure Research Laboratory Office of Research and Development, U.S. Environmental Protection Agency, Cincinnati, Ohio 45268, 10 p.

30

The appendix tables are in separate Excel files that can be accessed at *http://pubs.usgs.gov/of/2012/1142*.

Appendix A. Quality-Control Data for Water-Quality Samples

Table A1. Quality-control data from water-quality samples, Upper Klamath Lake, Oregon, 2009: Blank samples.

Table A2. Quality-control data from water-quality samples, Upper Klamath Lake, Oregon, 2009: Routine split samples.

Table A3. Quality-control data from water-quality samples, Upper Klamath Lake, Oregon, 2009: Replicate samples.

Table A4. Quality-control data from water-quality samples, Upper Klamath Lake, Oregon, 2009: Split sample interlaboratory measurements.

Table A5. Quality-control data from water-quality samples, Upper Klamath Lake, Oregon, 2009: Nutrient spiked samples.

Table A6. Quality-control data from water-quality samples, Upper Klamath Lake, Oregon, 2010: Blank samples.

Table A7. Quality-control data from water-quality samples, Upper Klamath Lake, Oregon, 2010: Routine split samples.

Table A8. Quality-control data from water-quality samples, Upper Klamath Lake, Oregon, 2010: Replicate samples.

Table A9. Quality-control data from water-quality samples, Upper Klamath Lake, Oregon, 2010: Split sample interlaboratory measurements.

Table A10. Quality-control data from water-quality samples, Upper Klamath Lake, Oregon, 2010: Nutrient spiked samples.

Appendix B. Data from Water-Quality Samples

Table B1. Data from water-quality samples, Upper Klamath Lake, Oregon, 2009.

Table B2. Data from water-quality samples, Upper Klamath Lake, Oregon, 2010.

Appendix C. Concentrations of Un-Ionized Ammonia in Water-Quality Samples

Table C1. Concentrations of un-ionized ammonia in water-quality samples, Upper Klamath Lake, Oregon, 2009.

Table C2. Concentrations of un-ionized ammonia in water-quality samples, Upper Klamath Lake, Oregon, 2010.

www.ingramcontent.com/pod-product-compliance
Lightning Source LLC
Chambersburg PA
CBHW080352290526
45791CB00009BA/2842